MW00627804

SCALPEL
MOMENTS

FLORIDA
HOSPITAL
Since 1908

SCALPEL
MOMENTS

BENJAMIN F. REAVES

Allowing God

to Remove What

Holds You Back

FLORIDA HOSPITAL

SCALPEL MOMENTS
Copyright © 2016 Benjamin F. Reaves
Published by Florida Hospital Publishing
605 Montgomery Rd, Altamonte Springs, FL 32714

TO EXTEND *the* HEALING MINISTRY *of* CHRIST

EDITOR-IN-CHIEF:	Todd Chobotar
INTERNAL PEER REVIEW:	George Guthrie, MD
	Michael Knecht, MDiv, MBA
	Sherri Grace
EXTERNAL PEER REVIEW:	Herman Davis, MDiv
	Patricia Rahming, RN, BSN
PROMOTION:	Caryn McCleskey
PRODUCTION:	Lillian Boyd
COPY EDITOR:	Pamela Nordberg
AUTHOR PHOTO:	Spencer Freeman
COVER DESIGN:	Dog-Eared Design
INTERIOR DESIGN:	Fudge Creative

For volume discounts please contact special sales at:
HealthProducts@FLHosp.org | 407-200-8224

Library of Congress Control Number 2016937801
Printed in the United States of America.
PR 14 13 12 11 10 9 8 7 6 5 4 3 2 1
ISBN 13: 978-0-9887406-2-4

For other life changing resources visit:
FloridaHospitalPublishing.com
CreationHealth.com

*Dedicated to the love of a lifetime
the late Jean Manuel Reaves
who for fifty-eight years
shared and supported
each step of the journey.*

Contents

SECTION 2: WHAT HOLDS YOU BACK

Editor's Note

FOR MORE THAN 50 YEARS Dr. Benjamin Reaves has served as a distinguished preacher, teacher, speaker, and leader. He is known the world over for his ability to challenge and inspire through his powerful messages. After many years of ministry work—in the pulpit, in academia, and in the corporate world—Dr. Reaves' words are being collected for the first time in book form.

If you've ever had the privilege of hearing a great sermon or experiencing a fantastic live presentation, you know there is an art to public speaking. It is an art that differs in several respects from the written word. While both forms of communication use words, sentences, and ideas to communicate their messages, the two styles can vary greatly. For instance, a dynamic speaker might employ tools such as: tone of voice, rhythmtg of speech, frequent theme repetition, contractions and truncated sentences. All to communicate to a live audience and add emotional context. The same message made in written form might use tools such as: headings and subheadings, longer sentences, less repetition, and more formal language.

Many of the chapters in this book were first presented as sermons or devotionals delivered by Dr. Reaves in his distinctive oral style. As far as possible, we have attempted to retain the rhythm, tone, and unique style of his spoken words, so that you can almost "hear" him speak through the pages of this book.

It is my hope that you will be blessed and inspired as you read Dr. Reaves' written words, just as thousands have been blessed by hearing him speak them.

Todd Chobotar
Publisher and Editor-in-Chief

Foreword

I CAN'T THINK OF ANYTHING THAT has been more of an honor than the opportunity to write the foreword to Dr. Benjamin Reaves' new book *Scalpel Moments*.

During my time as President and CEO of Adventist Health System, Ben and I worked closely together and he became a trusted counselor. He always gave me his best thinking on any issue, whether the comments brought good news or not. In my experience, Ben has unusual insight and wisdom to all issues, but especially those that touch on mission and the spiritual impact we have on those we serve. I believe what is true for me is true for many leaders within our company who count Ben as a very valued counselor.

For the book itself, I would first comment on the title—which I believe is ingenious. *Scalpel Moments* and the image it conjures is particularly potent considering the background from which the book is written. As Christian believers we know that Scripture makes it clear that the Holy Spirit can cut like a scalpel down to the marrow of our spiritual nature given at creation. By building on this understanding, Ben helped me gain deep insights into my own attitudes and thinking about spiritual matters.

Ben is a master storyteller. Page after page, he draws you in through his stories and you can hardly wait to see the lessons and precepts he calls forth. I find that making these points through concrete stories is the most powerful way to draw out moral lessons on how we as believers should conduct our day-to-day walk with the Lord.

The overall message of *Scalpel Moments* is quintessential Dr. Reaves. For anyone who knows him and looks back on the counsel and advice he has given, you will hear his voice in every story and every page of the book. I urge everyone to obtain a copy and immerse themselves in the book. You will receive a fresh dose of Ben's wisdom and the book will memorialize the kind of insight into spiritual matters that his own long walk with the Lord has produced in his life. This is one of those books you dare not fail to read and keep for future reference. I can imagine pulling it out in years to come to remind me of its vital lessons in the walk of life.

DON JERNIGAN, PhD
Author, *The Hidden Power of Relentless Stewardship*

If there is something, anything,
  that gets between you and God,
  then whatever it is,
  it needs to be cut away.
It needs a scalpel moment.

~ Dr. Benjamin Reaves

Introduction
WHAT ARE SCALPEL MOMENTS?

A SCALPEL, OR LANCET, IS A small and extremely sharp-bladed instrument used for surgery or anatomical dissection. It is designed to delicately cut and remove unwanted, unneeded, or dangerous growth in the body.

Though this is not a book on medical care, it is a book on spiritual care. There are those occasions in life that, frozen by the camera of reality, become one of those times that I call a "scalpel moment." These are those unexpected, unanticipated moments when an encounter, a word, a comment, a look, a realization, or a divine intrusion like an extremely sharp scalpel peels back layers taken for granted, rationalized—overlooked layers of attitude, options, choices, decisions, or behaviors. Layers that can hide the "better you."

Hence, the book in your hands. It is filled with stories of the things I have learned and experienced over a lifetime of God's grace. Stories of my mistakes, my failures, but also of some triumphs too. I've also included stories about what I have learned not only from my own "scalpel moments," but those of others— those whom I have known personally or whom I have read about in the pages of Scripture. Yes, Scripture is filled with people not so different from you and me, people like David, the apostle Peter, and others who had their moments "under the knife" as well.

However personal some of these stories are, they are also human stories containing human lessons, which is why I believe readers will find places where they can relate, where they can say, "I know just what he means here." But more than that, my hope and prayer for this book is that, as you read, you will learn, you will grow, and maybe when confronted or challenged, you will experience a "scalpel moment" of your own.

If so, then my work here will have been much more than worth it.

SECTION I:

*Allowing God
To Remove*

Is there something in your life that you would be better off without? What habits or life circumstances have you slipped into that are causing you pain? Have you ever wondered why each of us has experienced loss at one time or another and how it impacts each of us differently?

A scalpel moment can be one of painful awareness, disturbing clarity, sorrowful regret, disturbing recall. A scalpel moment can be a moment of positive awakening that can reveal, restore, renew.

While scalpel moments may be embarrassing, painful, distressing, and upsetting, they can also be the opportunity needed to reacquaint you with your better self.

That's why I also call them "moments of grace." Because they can be God's opportunity to show us His grace, to show us that, despite our faults and mistakes, He loves us, forgives us, and wants to give us the opportunity, by His grace, to change, to grow, to shed excess baggage.

Chapter One

SCALPEL MOMENTS

*G*OD, SEE WHAT IS IN MY HEART. *Know what is there. Test me. Know what I'm thinking. See if there's anything in my life you don't like. Help me live in the way that is always right." Psalm 139:23–24 (NIRV)*

It was one of those unusual moments. Chris Matthews, television host of *Hardball*, was interviewing Tony Snow, a White House presidential spokesman under George W. Bush. He was probing the controversial political attack ad on Harold Ford in Tennessee. The ever articulate Snow was reciting the excuse that the Republican Party had supplied the money to the group that made the commercial, but that because of legal intricacies, the party had no control over the airing of the ad.

The excuse came across like this: *Here's some money, do what you want with it because we have no relationship to it.*

When Snow finished the rather convoluted spin, Matthews concluded the conversation by saying, "You're doing your job, Tony, but you don't really believe that. You're better than that."

The expression that came over Snow's face revealed that the comment stung him deeply. Frozen by the camera, it became another "scalpel moment," a moment when a word, a comment, or a look like an extremely sharp scalpel peels back taken-for-granted or overlooked layers of attitude, option, or behavior.

I wonder if it was like the moment Peter experienced, recorded in the book of Acts. Peter visited the city of Antioch, acting in accordance with the light given from heaven, and overcoming his natural prejudice, and sat at the table with the Gentile converts.

But when certain Jews, who were zealous for the ceremonial law, came from Jerusalem, Peter injudiciously changed his deportment toward the converts from paganism and instantly stopped eating with them. Old habits die hard, don't they, especially when covered in the robe of a false righteousness?

This weakness on the part of a respected leader must have left a most painful impression on the minds of those Gentile believers. *Is this what our faith in Jesus is about?* But when Paul, every bit as faithful a Jew as Peter, saw the prejudice that Peter had exhibited, he rebuked him. He said, *Come on, Peter, I know you are better than that* (Galatians 2:13–14).

A scalpel moment for Peter, for sure.

The conviction of David's guilt was the saving of his soul.

Similar to the moment was when the prophet Nathan told the parable of the ewe lamb to the king. The parable of a rich man who would not take from his own flocks and herds to feed a traveler on his journey, but took from a poor man his one little female lamb which he dearly loved. David, not discerning the parable was about him, condemned the horrific acts. When David uttered the condemnation, Nathan replied, "You are the man."

Another scalpel moment, a moment when Nathan said to David, in so many words,

"David, you're better than that." And David was overwhelmed. He had not one word to say in his own defense. However painful to David, this experience was most beneficial. But for the mirror Nathan held up before him, in which he so clearly recognized his own likeness, David would have gone on, this sin remaining against him. The conviction of his guilt was the saving of his soul. He saw himself in another light, as the Lord saw him, and as long as he lived he regretted and repented of his sin.

David offers no excuses. He feels the sense of his sin. He does not seek to excuse his course or palliate his sin, but with sincere grief, he bows his head before the prophet of God and acknowledges his guilt.

Scalpel moments—we all have experienced them, haven't we?

It reminds me of a time when, while a student at college sitting at a table with some students, we were making fun of the appearance of a young lady at a nearby table. Unknown to me, at another table a friend of mine was observing. She touched my arm; I saw pain and disappointment in her eyes as she said, "Benny, I'm surprised you would do something like that. *You are better than that.*"

Another scalpel moment.

I can't speak for Tony Snow. Peter saw the error into which he had fallen and immediately set about repairing the evil that had been wrought, so far as was in his power. So did David, who, when confronted, uttered, "I have sinned against the Lord."

Scalpel moments can be moments in which we realize our faults and have the opportunity to change.

As for me, yes the years have passed. But I still remember the shame I felt. I've never forgotten her words to me.

Scalpel moments can also be moments of grace, moments in which we realize our faults and have the opportunity to change. Sometimes moments are highlighted by words or simply a look like a razor-edged scalpel to peel back layers of professional accumulation back to the real, better you. While scalpel moments may be embarrassing, painful, upsetting, the truth is they can be the opportunity needed to reacquaint you with your better self. Moments of grace that can lead to a heart petition, as of the psalmist in these beautiful words:

"Search me, O God, and know my heart; test me and know my anxious thoughts. Point out anything in me that offends you, and lead me along the path of everlasting life" *(Psalm 139:23–24, NLT).*

Chapter Two

BRASS FOR GOLD

"HOLLYWOOD IS BACK."

That headline hit *play* on the video recorder of my memory. Hollywood Henderson, that is.

On the football field he was a coach's dream: agile, mobile, and hostile.

Off the field he was a reporter's dream, the personification of the fast life until he faded from the headlines into drugs, and then prison. All of which was vividly captured in his painfully honest book, *Out of Control: Confessions of an NFL Casualty.*

Decades later Hollywood came back, but with a new book entitled *In Control: The Rebirth of an*

NFL Legend, where he recounted over twenty years of being clean and sober. It was the opposite of that first book, which was the story of a life gone wrong. The story of the loss, not just of fame, fortune, freedom, and family but of principles, standards, and values. Somehow we foolishly think of loss in terms of the material; however, material loss is the least part of the bankruptcy of life.

It was that first story of Hollywood's loss, *Out of Control,* that parallels a story found in the Bible about Rehoboam, son of Solomon, and one intoxicated by prosperity and power.

> Traits like honesty and integrity have become the hit-and-run victims of a moral recession.

"But when Rehoboam was firmly established and strong, he abandoned the Law of the Lord, and all Israel followed him in this sin. Because they were unfaithful to the Lord, King Shishak of Egypt came up and attacked Jerusalem in the fifth year of King Rehoboam's reign . . . So King Shishak of Egypt came up and attacked Jerusalem. He ransacked the treasuries of the Lord's Temple and the royal palace; he stole everything, including all the gold shields

Solomon had made" *(2 Chronicles 12:1–2, 9, NLT)*.

The three hundred golden shields symbolized the glory, the power, the prestige, and the prosperity with which God had blessed the obedience of His people.

Yet now the golden shields were gone, and along with them all the glory, power, and prestige they had symbolized as well.

Is there a warning here for us—a warning about the ever-present danger of losing the golden shields of purity, honesty, integrity, consecration, and commitment? If this is the warning, then it is so needed, especially in light of the fact that traits like honesty and integrity have become the hit-and-run victim of a moral recession. Disturbing reports of government officials, judges, bankers, priests, and ministers— leaders for whom surely there once was a day when the walls of their souls were hung with shields beaten out of the gold of honorable ambition, high ideals, and unquestioned integrity. And yet, somewhere and somehow, the gold is gone, and on the walls hang only empty hooks. In the flickering light of memory, we can all recall yesteryear or literally yesterday when the walls of our life temples were covered with golden shields.

But now compromise creeps in, hopes dim, enthusiasm deadens, and commitment dulls. And then somehow in the battle of life is the invasion of questionable motives, self-serving indulgences, deteriorating values, and eroding ideals. And soon we are left with nothing but our own empty walls.

But the story of Rehoboam doesn't end here. The next verse says: "King Rehoboam made shields of brass" *(2 Chronicles 12:10, KJV)*. Humiliated in defeat, embarrassed by the loss of the golden shields, Rehoboam commanded his artisans to make another three hundred shields of brass so that when he marched to the temple as Solomon had done before him, once more three hundred shields would gleam in the sun!

But the gold was gone, and all that remained was brass.

So then this could be a warning, not just about the danger of losing the golden shields, but also about the seductive temptation to substitute brass for gold, an ill-fated attempt to recapture what once was but to do so falsely and with wrong motives.

This can happen even in the life of a Christian organization when and if the reason for existence is overshadowed by the struggle to exist. It can be revealed in disguising ethical decline and mission decay, with spurious substitutes and with manufacturing the appearance of what no longer exists.

It happens in marriage, where flowers, candy, and gifts become the brass for the gold of love, honor, and faithfulness.

Is my commitment and character what it once was?

It happens in human relationships where artificial greetings, diplomatic handshakes, and frozen smiles mean nothing but just more brass for gold.

Yes, we may experience upward mobility, carry larger responsibilities, and enjoy impressive reputations with increasing influence. But the question persists: Is my commitment and character what it once was, or has the Rehoboam in you, and the Rehoboam in me, fashioned brass for gold?

This is a painfully insistent question that is not easily discussed, and one not easily dismissed. Have the golden shields been traded as down payments on success and in their place quietly hung brass substitutes that are pleasing to the public and soothing to the conscience?

If so, *and you realize that it is so,* then maybe you have reached a scalpel moment in your own life?

Then surely it is time for some cutting to be done.

Even though Rehoboam was concerned about the loss of the golden shields, his greatest concern was maintaining an illusion of a reality no longer existent. His concern was directed not at correcting, but camouflaging—with evasions, inconsistencies, indiscretions, and compromises.

He was creating illusions.

> People with integrity walk safely, but those who follow crooked paths will slip and fall.
> Prov. 10:9, NLT

Are we in the business of illusions? Living with an illusion is devilishly easy. After all, in the whirlwind of commendable activity, brass looks a lot like gold. In painful honesty it all really comes down to a personal challenge, that of acknowledging that which has been lost—and, instead of settling for substitutes, by God's grace reclaiming and renewing the gold of 24-carat commitment while God cuts away (your scalpel moment) all the dross.

Chapter Three

FACING FEAR

WHAT I REMEMBER IS THE fear, attempting to face the fear.

I remember when I was seven or eight, staying awake half the night because my grandfather's coat hanging on the door looked like someone in the doorway. My solution to the fear was to put my head under the covers. *If I couldn't see it, then it couldn't see me.*

Though that act was childish, at the age of seventy-four I almost repeated that experience. My wife had been hanging clothing on a rack and rolled the clothing rack into the hallway. Engrossed in my study, I forgot about the rack. When I turned out the light to go through the hall, fear enveloped me. *It looked like someone in the doorway.*

All of us have faced fear. The real issue, however, is *how* we face fear. Deny it, repress it, run away from it?

Peace is what I leave with you...Do not be worried and upset; do not be afraid.

John 14:27, GNT

Fear had been on my mind ever since the first day I noted hoarseness in my neck, a difficulty in clearing my throat. After three weeks I decided I would visit my physician. Things then moved swiftly. Following his exam he directed me to an ear, nose, and throat specialist. After use of his special instruments, the specialist informed me that my right vocal cord was paralyzed. At that moment I was face-to-face with fear that somehow the world had caved in. After all, I was a public speaker, a preacher, in demand with a calendar filled with appointments and additional invitations and requests. As I reflect, in a disturbing way my self-identity was closely tied to the popularity reflected by invitations coming from around the world. A lifetime of service seemed to be over. Even the twenty-one years as a featured speaker, along with Tony Campolo, John Claypool, John Killinger, and others on the renowned Chicago Sunday Evening Club seemed to be over.

Next I was directed by the specialist to a series of CT scans, which ruled out causal factors such as growths or lesions or tumors. However, they did reference an aortic aneurysm. Talk about fear: my father had succumbed to an aneurysm in the chest at the age of fifty-three!

For the next few days I faced the fear that my life as I had known it was over. As I look back on that time, I am saddened that I was so distraught over the loss of my voice that I failed to note that, if it hadn't been for the paresis, or paralysis, of my vocal cord, the dilation of my aorta would not have been noted and subjected to attentive monitoring.

During those days of tests and unresolved questions I found myself a frequent visitor to the land of midnight meditation. During those times a small verse took on mountainous proportions: "When I am afraid, I put my trust in you" *(Psalm 56:3 NIV)*.

Notice: it's *when* I am afraid, not *if* I am. And who is this talking of being afraid? King David, the famous giant killer. He was the one who, while others in fear ran from the giant, he ran toward the giant.

How did he do that? He gives the secret right in this text. "When I am afraid, I will put my trust and faith in you," says the same verse in the AMP. Or as the CEV puts it, "When I am afraid, I keep on trusting you." It must not be overlooked that along with David's trusting, he had his slingshot, the ammunition of selected stones, and the accumulated skill of persistent practice in slingshot marksmanship. However, his dependence was on God. "When I am afraid, I keep on trusting you."

It is true we are told that fear is a normal human emotional reaction, a built-in survival mechanism signaling us of danger and preparing us to deal with it. However, the Bible mentions two specific types of fear.

The first type is beneficial and is to be encouraged. It is the fear of the Lord. This type of fear is a reverential awe of God, a reverence for His power and glory. The second type is a detriment and is to be not only discouraged but, indeed, overcome. That fear, as one writer, Usman B. Asif, puts it, "is a dark room where negatives are developed."[1]

David H. Roper reminds us that "while Jesus doesn't condemn it, He doesn't want us to be crippled by it, so when Jesus said to His disciples, 'Do not be afraid' in each case he used a verb tense that suggests continuance. In other words, he told them, 'Don't keep on fearing.'"[2]

> I believe that God wants us to exercise our faith in the face of every fear-filled circumstance we face.

But, as we know, fear plays a major role in people's lives. All of us have fears. And, indeed, there's a lot of fear in this world too, isn't there? But most of the fears we carry around aren't big societal fears, such as of terrorism or war. They are, instead, the personal fears like finances (mortgages, debts, job loss) or sickness (cancer, heart attacks, strokes). It's a fear that is like "negative faith" and is based on doubt that God is still in control of things.

I believe that God wants us to exercise our faith in the face of every fear-filled circumstance we face, while evaluating every situation from the mindset that He is Lord over all things in heaven and on earth.

Yes, fear has been on my mind ever since that hoarseness in my throat, but like David I have discovered that there's nothing like the promises of God to enable us to face our fears.

Now, I can't recommend to you a hyped nasal spray that is supposed to treat the part of the brain that controls fear. You just spray this stuff into your nostrils and fear is supposed to go away. I have my doubts . . . On the other hand, I can testify of a divine promise for the heart, mind, and life, a promise in the Word of God which says: "So do not fear, for I am with you; do not be dismayed, for I am your God. I will strengthen you and help you; I will uphold you with my righteous right hand" *(Isaiah 41:10, NIV)*.

> The key to facing fear is total and complete trust in God.

And to that divine promise I responded like David, who wrote: "In God have I put my trust: I will not be afraid what man can do unto me" *(Psalm 56:11)*. What the psalmist is saying is that regardless of what happens, he will trust in God. This is the key to facing fear—total and complete trust in God. A trust that enabled me to return to the Chicago Sunday Evening Club television ministry and other opportunities for preaching. A trust that turned a period of fear into a scalpel moment.

What about you, can this be a scalpel moment in your life? A moment to face your fears in the power of God? A time to refuse to give in to fear and, instead, to turn to God even in the darkest times and trust in God to make things right, even if the outcome isn't what you want? A time to allow God to cut away the fears and replace them with trust, with the promise that He offers us?

This trust delivers from fear that freezes, and panic that paralyzes. This trust takes comfort in God's words: "Don't panic. I'm with you. There's no need to fear for I'm your God. I'll give you strength. I'll help you. I'll hold you steady, keep a firm grip on you" (Isaiah 41:10, MSG).

Seize this moment, this scalpel moment, and allow Him to not just cut out what needs to be removed but, with creative power and grace, fill you with faith and trust.

Chapter Four

Bring Me Up Samuel

"BRING ME UP SAMUEL."

Words from the Old Testament. Words to remember. Words heavy with a shadowed sadness. Words of one who crouches amid the wreckage of his life. Words by one hidden in disguise and cloaked by darkness.

In disobedience to God's clear command, he slinks to the cave of the witch of Endor. And there, in the midnight of his soul, he cries out in panic-edged desperation, "Bring me up Samuel. Bring me up Samuel." The cry of Endor's cave is a cry that cannot be forgotten because it has an incredible horror about it.

What is going on here? What is this cry and what can we learn from it?

Israel was a nation draped in mourning. Samuel the beloved prophet was dead. King Saul, terrified by the approaching armies of the Philistines, had inquired of the Lord in prayer but had received no answer.

> In the cry of Endor's cave
> we hear our own voices,
> in pained regret over
> opportunities lost,
> privileges neglected,
> and talents wasted.

"When Saul saw the Philistine army, he was afraid; terror filled his heart. He inquired of the Lord, but the Lord did not answer him by dreams or Urim or prophets. Saul then said to his attendants, 'Find me a woman who is a medium, so I may go and inquire of her.'"

"There is one in Endor," they said.

"So Saul disguised himself, putting on other clothes, and at night he and two men went to the woman. 'Consult a spirit for me,' he said, 'and bring up for me the one I name.'

"But the woman said to him, 'Surely you know what Saul has done. He has cut off the mediums and spiritists from the land. Why have you set a trap for my life to bring about my death?' Saul swore to her by the Lord, 'As surely as the Lord lives, you will not be punished for this.' Then the woman asked, 'Whom shall I bring up for you?' 'Bring up Samuel,' he said" *(1 Samuel 28:5–11, NIV)*.

If you put the scriptural videotape in reverse, it would have seemed like only yesterday when Saul—then in the morning of his life, blessed with marvelous privilege and magnificent opportunity—stood before the people as Samuel proclaimed, "God has anointed you to be prince over his people, Israel."

It would have seemed like only yesterday when, in humble disbelief, he heard Samuel proclaim to the people, "Do you see him whom the Lord has chosen? There is none like him among all the people."

It would have seemed like only yesterday when he heard the thunderous roar, "Long live the king! Long live the king!"

But now, in desperation, he seeks out a satanic source because the morning of his life had now become the midnight of his soul. The cry of Endor's cave rings out: "Bring me up Samuel. Bring me up Samuel."

How sad that now, now that Samuel was dead, Saul cries out for him. When Samuel lived as a prophet among them, Saul had ignored, disregarded, deceived, and rejected him. But now Samuel was dead. Now come words to remember, the haunting cry of Endor's cave. The cry for a ghost of a chance, "Bring me up Samuel."

But, in its own way, in that cry of Endor's cave we hear our own voices, in pained regret over opportunities lost, privileges neglected, and talents wasted. How many times have our cries gone up to the Endor cave of life?

As a former university professor, I remember Perry, a naturally gifted and personable student. He was focused on enjoying the social aspects of higher education. He spent the quarter disregarding assignments and skipping classes. But at the end of the quarter when grade time came, his cry went up from Endor's cave: "Can I have another chance? Can I have some grace? What about letting me do some makeup work? Can't you give me some extra credit?"

Bring me up Samuel.

Which is another way of saying, "I messed up, big time. Doc, can I have another chance?"

I think of families, and sometimes the cry of Endor's cave is the cry of a husband or a wife as the union of an immature mind and a hard head give way to harsh words that are met with bitter invective. When unrelenting stubbornness collides with pride set in concrete, then harsh, cutting words and hateful reactions result in a ruptured relationship. And all that is left is loneliness, pain, and bitter memories. Then comes the cry, "Bring me up Samuel."

> Good and evil both increase at compound interest. That is why the little decisions you and I make every day are of such infinite importance.
>
> C.S. Lewis

If I'd only been more patient. If I only had another chance.

It is no secret that at times the cry of Endor's cave is the cry of parents. Parents who have been so busy, working part time, full time, overtime, so busy that home has become a fast-food counter. Or a motel and a parking lot. And the one day they wake up to discover that they've been so busy giving their children something to live with (material things), they've given them nothing to live for. And, as they think about the really important things that they wanted to do, hot tears well up in their eyes, mountainous lumps choke their throats, and they cry out: "Turn back, turn back, turn back time in the flight. Make them children again, just for tonight."

Or, in other words, "Bring me up Samuel. Bring me up Samuel."

And it could also be the cry of children who know everything and cannot be told anything. Locked in their selfish cocoons they take their parents for granted, making great demands, giving little thanks. But there will come a day when those parental understanding eyes are closed and those loving hands are stilled, and devastated children wake up to what they have lost and to remorse, regret, and the cry of Endor's cave, "Bring me up Samuel."

The cry of Endor's cave is never more tragic than in the spiritual life where the cave receives the most calls because of some indiscrete action or careless association. The painful time comes when a fragile reputation is shattered, leaving only the fragments of remorse and regret. Then begins the nightmare of public knowledge and disgrace or private shame about habits that should have been discarded, practices that we knew needed to be changed.

If we come now to a scalpel moment and allow God to change us, to take away those things that don't belong, we can escape the painful path that leads to Endor's cave. Maybe now is the time to ask: God, what is there in my life that needs to be cut out so I won't make the kind of mistakes made here?

And a giant step on that path is to be willing to have God cut away an all too common trait: the refusal to accept responsibility.

> The problem with Saul, and the problem with too many of us, is we don't want to own our mistakes.

The Scripture is clear: in Saul's mind, he was never to blame about anything. The fault either belonged to David or to Jonathan or to Samuel or to the people. The responsibility was placed somewhere, anywhere, except where it belonged. Saul needed a scalpel moment, lots of them.

I always identified with the story told by Dr. Fredrick Samson about his son coming home from school on report card day. He noticed that his son kind of slipped in the house quietly and was about to go up the steps, so he called him and said, "Well, isn't it report card day?"

The boy mumbled something, so he responded, "Well, bring me your card, let me take a look at it."

The boy dragged himself into the room and grudgingly extended the card to his father. His father looked down the grades. The first ones looked pretty good, and then all of a sudden he saw a D.

"What is this?"

"Uh, looks like a D."

"What is this D doing on this card?"

"Uh, uh, the teacher, the teacher gave me that D. See, that's her handwriting. She wrote that D. That's her D."

Then Dr. Samson said, "No, son, that's not her D. She didn't give you that D. You made that D. She recorded your D. That's your D."

The problem with Saul and the problem with too many of us is we never want to admit that "I made that D. That is my D and there is no one else to blame." Because Saul denied his responsibility, step one led to step two. And that is the silly optimism that he could evade the consequences of his actions. He could play with fire and not get burned. He could carry coals in his bosom and not be scorched. How can you rationalize it? Why do you think God's going to let you get away with it? You can explain all you want, but if it is contrary to "thus saith the Lord," the choice will carry its consequences and you'll meet them one day. You can't keep on escaping and evading consequences.

> God offers us our own scalpel moments, or "moments of grace," that enable us to change.

Every time you neglect, reject, and put off, you are taking another giant step closer to the cave. The sad bit of truth is Saul's cry for "a ghost of a chance" was not for pardon for sin and reconciliation with God. Sadly, he wanted deliverance from his enemies.

But the glorious goodness of the gospel is, it doesn't have to be that way. God offers us our own scalpel moments, or "moments of grace" that enable us to change.

Scripture graphically records others who sinned in far uglier ways than Saul. What about King David, a hot-blooded adulterer, a cold-blooded murderer? Yet, as E. G. White wrote of David: "The conviction of his guilt was the saving of his soul."[3]

David, who after the scalpel moment when God used the prophet Nathan to peel back the layers of deceit, denial, and deception, thankfully testified in the Psalms:

"Oh, what joy for those whose disobedience is forgiven,

whose sin is put out of sight!

"Yes, what joy for those whose record the Lord has cleared of guilt" (Psalm 32:1–2, NLT).

And the inescapable fact is it's going to be one or the other outcome of a scalpel moment. The happiness of David, "the joy for those whose sin is forgiven."

Or, in contrast, we have the painful story of the scalpel moment for Saul whose cry, "Bring me up Samuel" revealed just how far he had gone in turning away from the Lord, tragically rejecting what could have been a pivotal moment of grace.

Chapter
Five

SOMETHING TO SHOUT ABOUT

PROMISES FILL THE AIR. Promises of carpet cleaners to miracle supplements to the promises of the call-in psychics who are going to help you get your life together. The promises of the get-rich entrepreneurs who promise you riches and assure riches for themselves, if you only follow their proven formula available at a modest price.

And then, of course, there are the promises of youthful campus life. I've seen them: the promises scrawled in letters and written on pictures after one quarter's acquaintance: "I am eternally yours"; "Forever true only to you" and the like.

As parents we, too, have joined the promise

brigade: promises to our children, promises to our spouses, promises of patience, and promises of presence.

And even promises to ourselves.

Well, fortunately, your promises and mine are not all the promises there are. For I'm told that in the Word of God there are three thousand five hundred seventy-three promises. That's right: three thousand five hundred seventy-three.

And they are wonderful promises, all of them. But, no doubt, the best of all is the promise of salvation in Jesus:

"For God so loved the world that he gave his one and only Son, that whoever believes in him shall not perish but have eternal life" *(John 3:16, NIV)*.

And then there's the promise of eternal security in Jesus:

"My sheep listen to my voice; I know them, and they follow me. I give them eternal life, and they shall never perish; no one will snatch them out of my hand" *(John 10:27–28, NIV)*.

Or this one, the promise of His providence:

"And we know that in all things God works for the good of those who love him, who have been called according to his purpose" *(Romans 8:28, NIV)*.

All things do what?

According to the promise, they "work[s] for the good of those who love him, who have been called according to his purpose." That's truly a wonderful promise, is it not?

> Paul's joy, purpose, and contentment were rooted in one of the greatest promises, "My God shall supply all your need."

All of these precious promises come from God. And they are all so full of hope for those who claim them. But as I look across the landscape of Scripture, out of all the promises in the Bible, one keeps resurfacing and clamoring for attention.

Read it for yourself:

"But my God shall supply all your needs according to his riches in glory by Christ Jesus" *(Philippians 4:19, KJV)*. Or as the Living Bible renders it: "And it is he who will supply all your needs from his riches in glory." Or as the Revised Standard Version says it: "And my God will supply every need of yours according to his riches in glory in Christ Jesus."

Now this verse, this magnificent verse, is the foundation upon which the entire epistle of

Philippians is built. And Paul's joy, his purpose, and his contentment were all rooted in this declaration, which is one of the world's greatest promises. A promise to shout about: "My God will supply every need of yours."

Why is this a promise to shout about? Because it is a personal promise.

What do I mean?

I watch the TV hucksters. I watch the politicians as the camera zooms in on the close-up and they stare into the camera, hoping to look into your eyes. And they personally promise you so many things.

But I don't know them, and they don't know me. There's nothing personal about it. But this text in Philippians is a personal promise; it begins with the words, "My God." My God shall supply your need. Not any God, not a God, not even the God in whom you happen to believe, but "My God."

Paul is being emphatically clear that he is not referring to the gods of the Greeks or the Romans or the Assyrians or the Babylonians. No, when Paul said, "My God," he was talking about the God he knew personally. It was, yes, a personal promise.

Paul's God was Jehovah. Paul's God was the God who had revealed himself to Paul personally.

Paul's God was Abraham's God, the God who called Abraham and promised that he would be a blessing to all men. Paul's God was David's God, the God who spoke to David the shepherd boy and made him a king. Paul's God was Jeremiah's God, who called Jeremiah to be a prophet while he was in his mother's womb. Paul's God was Isaiah's God, who called him and to whom Isaiah responded, "Here am I, Lord. Send me." And even though He was the God of all of these, yet Paul testifies in a singularly personal way that "He is my God."

If you don't get
everything you want,
think of the things you don't
get that you don't want.
Oscar Wilde

And the point is that for this promise to be meaningful, to be something to shout about, it has to begin with and continue with a personal relationship with Jesus Christ.

It's the personal relationship that matters, and my fear is that for so many that's the crucial element that is missing, especially in religious settings, where it is so easy to get caught up in a kind of "corporate" spirituality. The kind of environment where there's a lot of religion but little personal relationship with God. The bottom line is that the only thing that makes a real difference is a personal experience with Jesus Christ. The personal possessive, the first-person personal possessive "my," as in "my God," is of the utmost importance.

That's the difference between theory and reality. That's the difference between hearsay and experience. There's no such thing as a spiritual experience by proxy or by majority vote. We must discover personally and relate to God personally. And so the "my" in "my God" makes all the difference. The promise of Philippians 4:19 means nothing unless the personal relationship is established first.

And this is such a wonderful promise because amid all the bad news—crime, violence, fear, and terrorism—this promise explodes with the positive. After all, God says, "I will supply" what you need. That word "supply" means "I will fill up." What does that mean? It means the difference between pulling into the gas station and telling the man to put a dollar in or to fill it up. God says, "I will supply; that is, I will fill it full."

It's important, too, to keep in mind the people whom Paul was addressing. In speaking to the Philippians, Paul was addressing those who, having little themselves, nevertheless shared what they had with him. And because they were sharing what they had with him, Paul was able to give this promise that God was going to take care of their needs.

You're concerned and helpful about mine, so God's going to take care of yours.

Comparison is the thief of joy.
Theodore Roosevelt

Keep in mind that this underscores the truth that hands that are open to give are hands that are open to receive. Thus, with this background, when we look at the text we can see that Paul is not saying, "God might supply." He's not saying that God could supply or God is out to supply. No, he's saying that "my God *will* supply all your needs."

Note something else. Paul did not say God "will supply all your *wants*." He didn't even say all your desires. No, he said all your *needs*. And, remember, this is the Paul who wanted an ailment healed that God never healed. It was a *want*, not a *need*, and a big difference can exist between them.

So now a crucial thought is this: if God

has promised to supply my needs, I must understand that the interpretation of "needs" rests in a higher hand than in mine. This is important because it's so easy to turn our wants into needs, our desires into necessities, and thus to become dizzyingly confused over artificial wants and genuine needs.

At the beginning of the 20th century, the average American wanted seventy-two things, and considered eighteen of them important. Fifty years later, the average American had 496 wants, and considered 96 of those as necessary for happiness. And now advertising, television, and the media daily add to our "needs" because every time you turn on the television you see something that someone is saying you need. And even if they weren't telling you that, you're telling yourself, because even people of faith are not immune to the subtle effects of this psychology.

And we have developed some soft notions of what is required in life. For instance, think of the panic that comes when, well, the refrigerator is broken. Well, there was a time when there were no refrigerators. There was a time when you were fortunate to have an icebox.

And even worse than that—walk into an atmosphere of gloom and despair. What is wrong?

The television is not working. Patrick Henry pronounced, "Give me liberty or give me death"; most modern Americans are simply saying, "Gimme. Gimme me more money, give me more goods, give me more of the creature comforts of a Cadillac culture," and without restraint we parade behind the pied piper of planned obsolescence.

Painfully, I am reminded of the first car I owned. It was a brand new 1958 forest green Ford Fairlane 500. I had it for about two years and kept it in immaculate shape. It was all that a person could want, until I saw a new 1960 Ford Galaxie with distinctively different, broad, sweeping rear fins.

> The painful truth is that many
> of our lives are overgrown
> with the unimportant.

Caught up in the current of cosmetic change that swept me along, I traded up at a loss to have the newest fashion. My dumb decision was reinforced when I received a call a few nights later from the new owner of my forest green Ford. He called to inquire if something hidden was wrong with it. Since it was in such perfect condition, he couldn't understand why it had been traded in. I still get consumer heartburn thinking about it.

It's not just cars. Refrigerators are built with square corners and then the next year those corners are rounded; lapels are broad, reaching almost to the shoulders, and then the next year they are narrow. Skirts are long, then, Lord help us, they're short. Now they're long again and we parade along the path of planned obsolescence.

You think these changes happen by accident? Are you kidding? It is planned that goods will go out of style and that we must be in style. In addition, many of us follow the practice of financing our artificial wants. We will go into debt over artificial wants and then we'll look to God to supply our genuine needs. Maybe the only way God can help us get this thing straight is to stop bailing us out until we have gotten over our obsession with our wants.

Maybe it's time for a scalpel moment here? A time to take a look at some of the excess baggage: all the desires and wants you have turned into needs—needs that are dragging you down spiritually and financially.

The painful truth is that many of our lives are overgrown with the unimportant. Then, when these wants and whims surface to priority and we don't get them, we begin to wonder if we can count on God at all.

And that is the axiom of Christian faith that God delights to grant what we really need. Do you believe that? Now if you believe it, then if He hasn't granted it—could it be because we don't need it?

> Whenever I have a need, the Lord God of heaven brings all that heaven has to meet that need.

Could it be that perhaps our greatest need is to truly know our needs? But whatever we truly need—whether physical or spiritual, mental or moral, financial or circumstantial, whether it includes guidance or strength, comfort, health, courage, food, or employment, God will supply that need. Whatever we need, even if it's a need for forgiveness or for fellowship or for victory over temptation or for victory over fear, whatever you need, the promise is that my God will supply it.

Also, in the earlier part of the chapter, Paul focused on the provisions of the Philippians for him, for which he was grateful. But now he focuses on the provision of God, and he says, "And my God will fully satisfy every need of yours according to His riches in glory in Christ Jesus."

According to his riches in glory. This phrase opens up the exhaustless treasures of the divine love. God is going to supply your need, according to *His* riches and in glory. Now it doesn't say that He will supply your need out of His riches; it says that He's going to supply your need *according to* His unlimited riches. That is a big difference.

If you are walking down the street in New York, as I often used to, you will meet those who are requesting help. And not only on the street but even on the subway they come to you asking for help, for assistance. They weren't asking for a dime (the days of "gimme a dime for a cup of coffee" are gone) but for a handout of whatever they can get.

Now suppose sitting with me on that train was a multimillionaire, and the man approached and asked each of us for a dollar, and it happens that I just have one dollar. That's all I've got. But the millionaire has a big fat wallet full of money. I reach in my pocket and I give the man my dollar. That is, according to my riches, I gave him all I've got. But now the millionaire reaches in that big wallet and takes out a dollar. He's giving him something out of his riches. There is still more. Mine is limited by my lack of riches. That is all I have; whereas the millionaire's is not limited by a lack of riches.

Thus, when God says, "I'm going to supply your need," He is saying, "I am going to do that according to my riches." In other words, everything I've got, you've got, and my riches are limitless. For God's action in meeting our need is accomplished by a divine ability that is measured by the abundance found in His riches, and He's going to give "according to His unlimited, inexhaustible riches."

Thus, whenever I have a need, the Lord God of heaven brings all that heaven has to meet that need. He gives according to His riches. In other words, the source is inexhaustible. There's no end to it.

That means that when the things of this world dry up, we can still trust in the Lord and His riches toward us. For the text, the promise, tells me that when the banks fold, when the oil is gone, when the jobs vanish, God's account will be just as full and sufficient as it is right now because it is a source that is inexhaustible, and it will never run dry.

Let's look at the whole text again: "And my God will supply every need of yours according to His riches in glory in Christ Jesus."

Notice, He will supply all our needs "in Christ Jesus." For those of us who are in Christ Jesus, the treasures of God are right here. You don't have to go downtown and wait until the bank opens to make your application. The treasures are right here, right now. Just open your hands and your hearts and receive the riches that are available for us in Jesus Christ.

> ## For godliness with contentment is great gain.
> 1 Timothy 6:6, NIV

All that you will ever need is what you have in Jesus Christ. For my Lord doesn't give strength. He is strength. He doesn't give victory. He is your victory. He doesn't give sufficiency. He is your sufficiency. And that term "riches in glory in Jesus Christ" sums it up, all in Him.

During the Great Depression in the early 1930s, a panel of speakers, including the great attorney and professed atheist Clarence Darrow, were speaking to a group of people on Chicago's South Side. Most of these people were black; thus, the Depression hit them harder than most. Money, jobs were scarce. And as Darrow spoke, he pointed out the harsh reality of the tough times. And then as he summed up the woes of the people seated before him, he concluded by saying, "And yet you folks sing as only you can sing and the question is, 'What in the world do you have to sing about?'" And before the question hardly left his mouth, quick as a flash, a lady in the audience shouted, "We've got Jesus to sing about."

You can take the promise of an ever-present Jesus who can supply all that you need.

Take His check, because that's what D.L. Moody called it: "God's check." The name of the firm is "My God." The promise to pay is seen in the words "shall supply." The amount to be paid? "All your needs." The account against which the check is drawn? "His riches." The signature on the check? "Christ Jesus."

But there's one thing missing: the endorsement of our faith on the reverse side. You can't cash the check unless you're willing to sign, and signing means being submissive to God's plan and providence for your life. Signing means trusting that God knows your needs. Signing means trusting that God will supply your needs as He sees fit. Signing means submitting to God's scalpel moments when they come.

Chapter Six

JESUS PASSING BY

I WANT TO LOOK AT THREE different stories about Jesus, three stories that I think can teach us something important about life. These are three vignettes, which, like transparencies, when combined or layered on each other, form a fleshed-out portrait of particular meaning and significance.

The first one is found in one verse: "As Jesus passed on from there, He saw a man named Matthew sitting at the tax office. And He said to him, 'Follow Me.' So he arose and followed Him" *(Matthew 9:9)*.

This is Jesus, passing by on just another day when Jesus, like on so many other days, passed by the tax collector's booth, the booth where Matthew, the tax collector, always sat. Day after ordinary day people grudgingly stopped at the booth to pay their hated taxes to the hated tax collector, who was nothing more than the physical object of their hate because he represented the oppressive might of Rome.

Jesus was most concerned with living a pure, transparent life of simple love and helpfulness.

But it was different with Jesus. He saw something of worth in this despised man, something the people could not or would not see. Jesus saw something here, and how glad we are that Jesus did because, to this day, we have the wonderful gospel of Matthew, which reveals to us so much about Jesus.

Second story:

"Now as Jesus passed by He saw a man who was blind from birth. And His disciples asked Him, saying, 'Rabbi, who sinned, this man or his parents, that he was born blind?'

"Jesus answered, 'Neither this man nor his parents sinned, but that the works of God should be revealed in him. I must work the works of Him who sent Me while it is day; the night is coming when no one can work. As long as I am in the world, I am the light of the world.'

"When He had said these things, He spat on the ground and made clay with the saliva; and He anointed the eyes of the blind man with the clay. And He said to him, 'Go, wash in the pool of Siloam' (which is translated, Sent). So he went and washed, and came back seeing.

"Therefore the neighbors and those who previously had seen that he was blind said, 'Is not this he who sat and begged?'" *(John 9:1–8).*

Here again, Jesus passing by. Jesus passing by on the road that He had traveled many times, only this time, as Jesus passed by, He met a man who had a great need. He had spent a lifetime groping his weary way along the twisting lanes and narrow streets day by day. He lived in a world of total darkness. Didn't know light, didn't know color, didn't know the look of a smile or the beautiful colors of a lily.

And the people didn't notice him because his presence was so familiar. Besides, no one had time or wanted to bother with a blind beggar. If they did, it was simply to toss him a crust to get rid of him.

As Jesus passed by, He saw him, the blind beggar; and so Jesus stopped and gave to the sightless man sight. He gave the man hope and He showed the man a love that he had never known before.

Jesus showed a love that had never been known before.

Third story:

"Then Jesus entered and passed through Jericho. Now behold, there was a man named Zacchaeus who was a chief tax collector, and he was rich. And he sought to see who Jesus was, but could not because of the crowd, for he was of short stature. So he ran ahead and climbed up into a sycamore tree to see Him, for He was going to pass that way. And when Jesus came to the place, He looked up and saw him, and said to him, 'Zacchaeus, make haste and come down, for today I must stay at your house.' So he made haste and came down, and received Him joyfully" *(Luke 19:1–6).*

Jesus, passing by, saw what might have been an ordinary thing: just a man in a tree. Trying to get a view over the crowds that always surrounded the master, this man had climbed the tree to get a better view of this stranger from Nazareth. Jesus, passing by, called to Zacchaeus and asked if He could dine with him at his home. Jesus invited himself to dinner. That unlikely meeting changed the whole world for the enormously wealthy Zacchaeus, to the point where the greedy and grasping man blurted: *I give half my possessions to charity and if I have cheated anyone I am ready to repay him four times over.*

What is it about these transparencies of biblical narrative when placed over each other that form a portrait perspective of the Master? What is the common thread through these stories that should speak to us?

First, all of these texts speak of Jesus. That would be significance enough. All of these texts speak of people whose lives were impacted by Jesus. Surely that would merit all our attention and speak to our deepest experiences.

And yet all of these texts speak of Jesus *passing by*, *passing through*, *passing along* in what could seem like just an ordinary way, just as you or I might be passing along the street or the hallway or off the elevator or through the mall, or the hotel, or the airport, or the ward, or office.

The impressive truth is that many of the greatest things that happened in the lives of people happened as Jesus passed along. Actually, He did most of his greatest deeds of kindness, performed most of His wondrous acts of mercy, and spoke most of His beautiful and enduring words of grace and hope *as He passed by* these people.

It's easy, of course, to do a good deed when you plan for it. It's easy to speak kind words when you plan for it, when you think about it beforehand, such as sending birthday or anniversary greetings to your friends.

But it is a different and usually a much more revealing thing to do a good deed on the spur of the moment. Saying some generous and heartening word as you bump into a person on a street corner quite unaware as you pass by. That's the real test of character—the unplanned acts of charity, the spontaneity, the gracious overflow of casual, unplanned love.

Just as the thoughtless unplanned word is indicative of our character, so is the unplanned act of love and caring.

Some people have a difficult time with the humdrum of ordinary days. They are blind to the promise of ordinary days. They are blind to the promise of the ordinary and have eyes only for the hour of excitement at the center stage of the prominent moment.

Days of crisis are not the testing days of courage, compassion, and caring. The test lies in the ordinary days, when the commonplace stretches and yawns from dawn till dusk. When you are just passing by.

Passing by is easy; stopping along the way to help others—that's harder.

Jesus, as He passed along, casually going here and there in a perfectly natural way and without a preconceived plan, did His works of love and spoke His words of tenderness and power.

Little bits of conversation or comment or stories dropped here or there. Great deeds of mercy and healing not planned in advance. Passing by an ill man, hearing a cry of need and responding to that need.

One might think that Jesus was absorbed in the big things, the big matters: how to meet and outwit His enemies, facing the final conflict, etc. But apparently Jesus was most concerned with living a pure, transparent life of simple love and helpfulness, passing by doing good.

Prominent here is the outgoing, spontaneous goodness of Jesus to the discouraged. He spoke words of hope, performing miracles of grace and love as He passed by.

We like to repeat that our mission takes us into the footsteps of Jesus. Hear his voice saying, "I have set you an example; you are to do as I have done for you."

> Nothing is more important than people, and if people are in need and we are there, we are called to help.

But that's not always easy, is it? We are often in a hurry. We have places to go, things to do, appointments to make. Passing by is easy; stopping along the way to help others—that's harder.

That's when we need the scalpel moments in our lives.

That's when we need to remember that nothing is more important than people, and if people are in need and we are there, we are called to help, even if it costs us something, even if means we have to sacrifice or have something cut from our lives.

It was on a cold November night in Times Square, Officer Lawrence DePrimo was working a counterterrorism post when he encountered an older, barefooted homeless man. The officer disappeared for a moment, then returned with a new pair of boots, and knelt to help the man put them on.

The act of kindness would have gone unnoticed and mostly forgotten, had it not been for a tourist from Arizona who took a picture. Seeing that picture was a scalpel moment for thousands who were reminded that beneath the layers of urban callousness are caring hearts.

That's why passing by, like Officer DePrimo, can indeed offer us some wonderful opportunities, not only to serve but to be blessed by the act of serving as well.

Chapter Seven

THE BURNING BUSH

THE SUN ROSE, AS USUAL, IN A dull haze over the endless expanse of sand. As it climbed in a cloudless sky, long shadows were cast over the wilderness with its savage crags. The sheep lay panting under the shadow of a great rock, or browsed as usual on the scant vegetation.

It seemed like any other hot desert day, except for this:

"And the Angel of the LORD appeared to him in a flame of fire from the midst of a bush. So he looked, and behold, the bush was burning with fire, but the bush was not consumed. Then Moses said, 'I will now turn aside and see

this great sight, why the bush does not burn'"
(Exodus 3:2–3).

A bush on fire was not uncommon in dry, hot desert country. Thorn bushes full of resin and sap occasionally burst into flames, the result of spontaneous combustion.

However, any ordinary fire would have flashed through, leaving only ashes, but this thorn bush was not consumed, not even scorched.

Moses was seeing a miracle.

There are days in all our lives that come unannounced, unheralded, but as we look back we realize they were monumental, the turning points of our existence. Such was the day that Moses was having.

"So when the LORD saw that he turned aside to look, God called to him from the midst of the bush and said, 'Moses, Moses!' And he said, 'Here I am'" *(Exodus 3:4, KJV).*

That voice that spoke, then, still speaks to those whose hearts are open to hear. The God of the bush that spoke to Moses then has a message from the bush for us now.

In this scene, as throughout Scripture, fire is an emblem of deity, a symbol of the power of God. And so the burning bush was another expression of the Lord. The drawing power of the bush rested in the fact of the fire that symbolized God's presence in the bush.

> God was trying to get across to Moses that even in his inadequacy, the power is in the presence.

What can we learn from this story for ourselves, today?

First, the Lord wasn't doing this for fun. No, He had a specific message for Moses. As the rest of the chapter reveals, God had a work for Moses to do. Moses had doubts about his abilities. Who was he that the people would listen to him? Besides, he couldn't really talk well, either. "Then Moses said to the LORD, 'O my Lord, I am not eloquent, neither before nor since You have spoken to Your servant; but I am slow of speech and slow of tongue'" *(Exodus 4:10)*.

Actually, Moses was right. What he said was true. He was honest. He was inadequate. That's a word we are uncomfortable with. With our great desire for competence, we always want to appear to be on top of things, have them under control. It's unsettling for us to realize that we are inadequate, as was Moses. But God was trying to get across to Moses that even in his inadequacy, the power is in the presence.

Moses needed to understand that before he could be sent, he needed an experience. A vision of the glory and power of God was an essential prerequisite. Moses needed to know, as we often need to be reminded, that the bush he turned aside to see was special, but only because there was fire in the bush. That means the power is in the presence.

Don't miss the point. Even though Moses had that bush experience, he still made excuses.

Most of us have all sorts of excuses, don't we? We retreat from risk on the basis of being too young or old. We have infirmities, physical or emotional, real or imagined. We have too many responsibilities or not enough.

Moses needed to be made conscious of the divine commission to his work. He needed a scalpel moment, a moment to realize that the power wasn't in him, but in God. After he uttered his excuse, what did the Lord say to him? "Who has made man's mouth? Or who makes the mute, the deaf, the seeing, or the blind? Have not I, the LORD? Now therefore, go, and I will be with your mouth and teach you what you shall say" *(Exodus 4:11–12)*.

Come on, Moses, you are better than that. I am not asking you do to this alone. I will be there with you. Live your faith, son!

Unfortunately, some of us are confused, sadly confused. We think God's commission comes to us "because of," when actually God's commission is "in spite of." Our priority preparation needs to be the awareness that, yes, God knows our faults, weaknesses, and shortcomings but is still willing to use us "in spite of" them.

May the God of hope
fill you with all joy and peace
as you trust in him.

Rom. 15:13, NIV

The power is in the presence, the presence of God and the reality of His great power to work in our lives.

While our plans, projections, and preparations give us facility and efficiency, we are totally dependent on the power that is in the presence. And the thrilling truth is the presence is not reserved for or limited to special days, high and holy days like conferences, convocations, or rural gatherings known as camp meetings. The presence can be known, felt, and experienced even in the desert of your daily routine—when it seems the dullness of the daily will crush you.

One of life's most common experiences is the letdown. After peak days like a graduation, a wedding, or a promotion come the humdrum, ordinary days again with the inevitable letdown. Some people seem to have considerable difficulty accepting this fact of human experience. They refuse to adjust themselves to it and consequently live miserable lives while yearning for hours of excitement in which they can take the center of the stage and bask in the glory of it.

Never be afraid to trust an unknown future to a known God.

Corrie ten Boom

Now this same fact of human experience is a part of man's religious life, too. In life's journey of the soul, there are luminous moments of inspiration when God seems near and real. But those moments are always followed by a letdown. And if ever you are going to be tempted to lose faith in God, nine times out of ten it will not be in moments of crisis when action or unusual courage is demanded but, rather, in what the mystics call the "dry periods." These are the days when nothing much happens and God seems far away and unreal. That is the peril of ordinary days, because it is then that it is easiest to lose faith in God.

Nor does it matter how we feel. Moses didn't feel up to the task. You will say that you don't feel very much like a child of God with your hands in the dishpan or up to your elbows in car grease. But it doesn't matter how you feel.

> We ought to trust Him as children and obey even if we don't always see where it's getting us.

If religion were dependent upon how you feel, it would be full to the brim one day and empty the next. It would be empty precisely when you need it most! It doesn't matter how you feel, or what other people think about you, or even what you think about yourself. All that really matters is what God thinks of you. And if He thinks of us as His children, then we ought to trust Him as children and obey even if we don't always see where it's getting us.

Even in the desert of your everyday existence,

God is saying that the place you are standing is holy ground, whatever the responsibility: nurse, teacher, administrator, parent. There is holy ground in the desert of the daily. Be faithful, trust in the Lord, allow Him to use the scalpel on our soul, and you will experience the reality of His presence and, who knows, what He will be calling you to do next.

Chapter Eight

MIND YOUR OWN BUSINESS

EVER HEAR THE WORDS, "MIND your own business"? It's usually an insult, is it not? We don't usually like to hear it either, do we?

But I'd like to offer a Bible text that could help us place this concept in another context: "You will keep him in perfect peace, whose mind is stayed on You, because he trusts in You" (Isaiah 26:3).

Clearly, in the world we live in, a concern for peace is more than appropriate. It's absolutely essential. I don't need to belabor the fact that, whether thinking globally, nationally, corporately, or personally, we are in need of peace.

And this need is addressed by this passage because it lays out what I call the "Organizational Chart for Peace." It identifies two areas of responsibility.

> Peace is not the absence of something, but the presence of Someone.

The first area of responsibility: keeping in perfect peace is *God's* business. Sometimes we get confused and so, occasionally, we need the following reminder, which comes from an anonymous quotation: "Good morning, this is God! I will be handling all your problems today. I will not need your help—so have a good day."

Yes, we need to be reminded that keeping us in perfect peace is God's business.

But then the other area of responsibility, this is our business: "Keeping your mind stayed on Him." Your business is to stay focused on Him. The rest is His business.

So, indeed, *mind your own business*. As some organizational wisdom would say, "Stay in your lane."

Now this idea can be taken to the extreme. A college president was awakened in the middle of night by the shrill ringing of the phone. He answered testily, "Who is this? What do you want?"

On the other end, the person excitedly informed him one of the buildings on campus was on fire. To which the president curtly responded, "Why are you calling me? Call the fire department!" slamming down the phone as he went back to sleep.

Now that is extreme, and it is not what I'm talking about. Minding your business is keeping your mind stayed on Him. And it is your choice. Choose to trust His keeping power. Keeping your "mind stayed" means constant trust, or habitual dependence, because there are constant challenges, pressures, and difficulties.

In this context, I had another scalpel moment.

It was my senior year in college, and the funds I needed for graduation were tied up. It was after my father had died, and because he had no will, the estate had gone into probate court. Burdened, I walked around discouraged, almost depressed at the loss of my dad and now the seeming loss of my education. My mother walked in while I was moping and asked, "Why haven't you packed your trunk? Where is the faith you preach about? Pack; it's your turn to practice what you preach."

Talk about a scalpel moment! Her words hit right to the center of my soul. She was saying to me, in motherly love, *Mind your business, do what you can do, and God will mind His.*

He did, unexpected funds were posted to my account, I completed my senior year, and graduated. Thus, I can testify it is not a possibility; it is a promise: God will mind His business, bringing peace.

> We need to be reminded that keeping us in perfect peace is God's business.

Often we mistakenly see peace as the absence of something, but, in fact, peace is not the absence of something but, instead, *it is the presence of Someone.* Peace is not determined by the conditions around but the presence within. Not just temporary, fleeting, brief periods of peace but perfect peace, complete peace, holistic peace, the peace that God brings when we mind our own business and let Him do His.

Chapter Nine

COLLISION WITH THE FAMILIAR

I T WAS DISCONCERTING, TO SAY the least. What I anticipated would be a homiletical slam-dunk could be described only as a head-on collision with the familiar. More on that in a second.

The familiar passage, embraced and revered by millions, grows out of a scene set in the cool morning air. Jesus and His disciples had withdrawn to the mountain where they had spent the day. The disciples listened to the timeless words found in Matthew 6, the Sermon on the Mount. The challenging words provided the core and the distillation of Jesus's teaching.

In those words, Jesus reminds His hearers of the substance and the aim of life. Again and again, He lifts up two general aspects of life: the spiritual and the material. He confronts His hearers, then, with choice and priorities: Seek Him and His kingdom, first laying up treasure in heaven and not on earth. And then be free from anxiety.

That sums up the familiar.

As for the collision—it is with an aspect of the familiar, something that I had evidently overlooked, misinterpreted, neglected, or ignored.

Those verses where He states, take no thought of clothes, food, etc. caught my attention. No problem, but in verse 35, the phrase, "Do not worry about tomorrow" is what so disturbed me.

Here, in the Lord's own words: "But seek first the kingdom of God and His righteousness, and all these things shall be added to you. Therefore do not worry about tomorrow, for tomorrow will worry about its own things. Sufficient for the day is its own trouble" *(Matthew 6:33–34)*.

Why did it disturb me? Because, frankly, it seems to go against the way I'm wired. It cuts across my history, even. I have, in all humility, prided myself on looking ahead, looking down the road. Having a focus on the future. Over the years I've had an intimate attachment with this because of the strong, even overwhelming desire to always be on top of my game.

> No good work is ever done while the heart is hot and anxious and fretted.
>
> Olive Schreiner

Comically and sadly, this overflowed into an obsession that reared its ugly head as the plane on which I was traveling was about to land. As the landing announcement was made, my mind went into high gear, planning my positioning with one foot already in the aisle, and on how I would be the first to stand and swivel into the aisle before anyone else. Thus, not only would I block everyone behind me, I could get my bags out of the overhead bin first and be ready to move down the aisle.

To compound my obsession, when I encountered others who were not as obsessed as I, worrying or thinking about the future, I made negative judgments about them, such as that they were just not on top of it (as I was), or that they just did not understand life and its grab bag of surprises. However the collision with the familiar, "Do not worry about tomorrow" forced me to rethink my attitude.

Was I obsessed with being first in the aisle, first to anticipate what might occur down the line, first to see what might happen tomorrow, first to detect unintended consequences? The text made me think about it.

I'd like to say it was a scalpel moment on the plane, but at the time while it could have been, it wasn't. It should have been, but only later did I realize what I needed to learn in that collision with the familiar, "Do not worry about tomorrow."

What did Jesus mean with that text, which is so familiar yet so profound?

Jesus is not advocating a shiftless, reckless, thoughtless attitude to life. Rather, He is forbidding a careworn, worried fear, which takes the joy out of life.

Be clear. Thought or forethought—in the sense of reflection, consideration—is required alike by Scripture and common sense. So again, that text does not mean: make no preparations for tomorrow's needs. For almost everything that is worth doing requires some forethought and planning and preparation.

Of course, as human beings we are future-oriented people, and most of us worry about tomorrow. I feel comfortable calling it "planning" or "anticipating." The Wayne Gretzky Syndrome, which is this: a good hockey player plays where the puck is; a great hockey player also plays where the puck *is going to be*.

This is fine and important, but it does present the challenge that this future focus often causes us to manufacture problems for tomorrow that never occur.

Be anxious for nothing, but in everything...let your requests be made known to God.

Phil. 4:6

Do not worry about your life. Jesus intended to free His disciples from worry. They were to live a day at a time, trusting God for their daily bread and leaving tomorrow in His hands.

Of course, that's easier said than done, right?

Ever hear the phrase: "Today's mercies for today's troubles"? It means today's mercies are not designed to carry tomorrow's burdens. Today's mercies are for *today's* burdens.

When I was younger, I didn't worry about tomorrow. I was too busy having fun today. However, as I age, I am more and more like the little seven-year-old girl who was thrilled when her dad took her to Disney World for the first time. She headed straight for Space Mountain. The dad worried that the roller coaster would be too scary for her. But she insisted.

To her delight, they rode it twice.

The next year they returned to the Magic Kingdom, and the daughter, now eight, again dragged the dad to Space Mountain. As they stood in line, though, the dad could see her soberly studying the signs that warned about the ride's speed.

"Dad," she blurted out, "I don't want to go on the ride."

The dad then asked her why she didn't want to go on it, since she had enjoyed herself so much last year.

She replied, "This year, I can read."

It's that way with me: the older I get, the better I can read the warnings about tomorrow.

What will become of our health? Will we go blind or deaf or lose our memories? Who will take care of us? What about tomorrow? Will we have the strength to live tomorrow when it comes, and to live it well and wisely and even joyfully?

The point? The strength to live tomorrow will be given tomorrow, not today. My task today is not to have the strength needed for tomorrow's burdens. My task today is to live by the mercies given for today, and to believe that there will be new mercies for tomorrow.

Worrying is like a
rocking chair. It gives you
something to do but
doesn't get you anywhere.
Anonymous

I can't express how critically important I believe this is for the living of the Christian life: for me, for you, for young adults in the work world, for middle-aged people facing major life changes, for older people with tremendous uncertainties before them. Foresight and foreboding are two different things. In the passage, foresight is commanded; foreboding is forbidden. So the point of Matthew 6:34 is not, *Don't make wise preparations*; the point of the passage is, *Don't bring the troubles and uncertainties of carrying out those preparations for tomorrow, into today.*

"Sufficient for the day is its own trouble."

Isn't that true enough?

You can know some of the pressures that are coming tomorrow. And part of your job may be to make some preparations for them. But how those preparations will turn out tomorrow and whether you feel strong enough today to do your part tomorrow—that is not something God wants you to carry today. Those are tomorrow's burdens. God does not give mercies today for bearing tomorrow's burdens.

Anxiety does not empty
tomorrow of its sorrows;
it empties today
of its strength.

Dwell on these words:

"Through the LORD'S mercies we are not consumed,

Because His compassions fail not.

They are new every morning;

Great is Your faithfulness."

(Lamentations 3:22–23).

It's the phrase "they are new every morning" that gives this great confidence that each day's mercies are given specifically for that day. They are "new" because yesterday's mercies were for yesterday's burdens. Today's mercies are for today's burdens. Hence they are new every morning.

While we may want the feeling of adequacy today for what we will have to go through tomorrow, God says, *Trust Me. I will give it to you when you need it.* "As your days, so shall your strength be" *(Deuteronomy 33:25)*.

Or listen to these words here, from Peter: "Cast all your anxiety on him because he cares for you" *(1 Peter 5:7, NIV)*. It does not say that you will never feel any anxieties to cast onto God. It assumes that *you will* have anxieties. That's the point! But the issue is how you deal with them. Anxiety does not empty tomorrow of its sorrows; it empties today of its strength.

The real problem behind anxiety is unbelief in the promises of God. We can battle the unbelief of anxiety only with the promises of God.

When I am anxious about some risky new venture or meeting, I battle unbelief with the promises: "Fear not, for I am with you; be not dismayed, for I am your God. I will strengthen you, Yes, I will help you, I will uphold you with My righteous right hand" *(Isaiah 41:10)*.

When I am anxious about being too weak to do my work, I battle unbelief with the promise of Christ: "My grace is sufficient for you, for My strength is made perfect in weakness" *(2 Corinthians 12:9)*.

When I am anxious about decisions I have to make about the future, I battle unbelief with the promise, "I will instruct you and teach you in the way you should go; I will guide you with My eye" (*Psalm 32:8*).

When I am anxious about facing opponents, I battle unbelief with the promise, "If God is for us, who can be against us?" *(Romans 8:31)*.

When I am anxious about getting old, I battle unbelief with the promise, "Even to your old age, I am He, And even to gray hairs I will carry you! I have made, and I will bear; Even I will carry, and will deliver you" *(Isaiah 46:4)*.

When I am anxious, fearful that I may make a shipwreck of my faith and fall away from God, I battle unbelief with the promise: "Being confident of this very thing, that He who has begun a good work in you will complete it until the day of Jesus Christ" *(Philippians 1:6)*.

We can battle the unbelief of anxiety only with the promises of God.

When we have an adequate knowledge of God, and if we have a personal relationship with God but we still worry, then it is because we have chosen the wrong focus. We have chosen to worry instead of trust.

I find that worry is easier to do when related to professional life, where my skills and talents and gifts come into play. But when it comes to health emergencies, I know I'm *way, way* out of my league. Here, I have to give them over to God, or the worry itself (never mind the health issue) would kill me. This reality came sharply into focus when after concluding a Sabbath sermon and walking down the aisle, I said to the pastor of the church, "I will not greet at the door; I'm going directly to the study." By the time I reached the study, chest pain was building and I was drenched with perspiration. With the help of my son-in law I reached the ER, and they swiftly rolled me into the operating room for cardiac bypass surgery. In those bewildering moments I clearly realized my crisis situation and my human limitation and earnestly confessed: "Lord, I'm in your hands." *In His hands, believing His promises and trusting His providence.*

Yes, as Jesus said, "But seek first the kingdom of God and His righteousness, and all these things shall be added to you. Therefore do not worry about tomorrow, for tomorrow will worry about its own things. Sufficient for the day is its own trouble" *(Matthew 6:33–34).*

Jesus began the verse with the word "but,"

connecting these thoughts with the great promises that came before. And it is because of the previous promises that you don't have to worry about tomorrow.

Live one day at a time.

> The mind that is anxious about future events is miserable.
> Seneca

Planning for tomorrow may be part of today's concern, but worry about tomorrow is not. That was the challenge for Jean and me when, after the birth of our only son, a solemn-faced Doctor Brayshaw gave us the news no parents want to hear. With careful words he informed us our son had been born with a hole in his heart wall. Tears and fears surfaced for both of us. Sympathetically, Dr. Brayshaw shared with us he would refer us to a pediatric cardiologist. During the days before the appointment, worried days and sleepless nights burdened us. In our visit with the specialist, he reinforced the gravity of the matter and the limited options. In desperation we did what a loving heavenly father invites us to do, taking and leaving our burdens with the Lord.

The Great Physician took charge of the case and the healing protocol. Praise God, some fifty years later, a healthy Benjamin Jr is evidence to take your burdens and worries to the God who hears and answers prayers.

God's invitation is to live one day at a time, being secure in the continuing presence of the divine physician, our provider who will be with you, leading you, helping you, strengthening you daily.

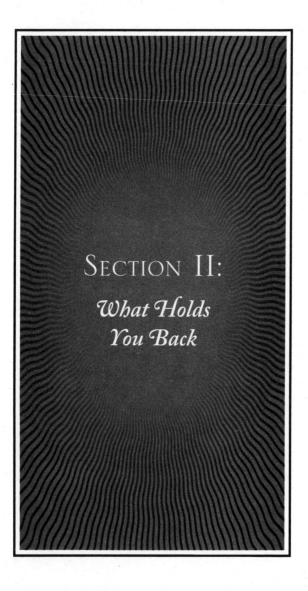

SECTION II:

What Holds You Back

As the stories from Section I have shown, trusting in God isn't always so easy. Sometimes it takes a scalpel moment to help us get our priorities straight and to make us realize that we can't do it on our own.

But trusting in God is only part of what it means to know Jesus. Another part is living the Christian life; that is, manifesting in our daily existence the faith that dwells in our hearts.

That's not always so easy, either. Sometimes we need scalpel moments to peel back layers of callousness or to cut away the things that keep us from doing as we should. The apostle Peter is one great example. When, just before the cross, Jesus said, "All of you will be made to stumble because of Me this night" (Matthew 26:31), Peter cried out, "Even if all are made to stumble because of You, I will never be made to stumble" (Matthew 26:33). And when Jesus said, right afterward, that before the rooster crowed Peter would have denied him three times, Peter declared: "Even if I have to die with You, I will not deny You!" (Matthew 26:35).

And, yet—what happened? Amid the turmoil of Christ's arrest, when the leaders took Jesus away, what did Peter do? First, as did all the other apostles, he fled. Scripture then says that, as he was waiting outside in the courtyard while Jesus was being interrogated inside, people who claimed that Peter was one of Jesus's followers confronted him. This happened not once, not twice, but three times.

Scripture describes the third time like this:

"And a little later those who stood by came up and said to Peter, 'Surely you also are one of them, for your speech betrays you.' Then he began to curse and swear, saying, 'I do not know the Man!' Immediately a rooster crowed. And Peter remembered the word of Jesus who had said to him, 'Before the rooster crows, you will deny Me three times.' So he went out and wept bitterly" (Matthew 26:73–75).

A scalpel moment, for sure.

If you know the Bible, you know that Peter became a new person after this bitter experience—an experience that enabled him to better live the life that he had been called to in Christ.

And, thus, the following stories, each with their own scalpel moments, tell about how people have learned, sometimes the hard way, about what it means to be a Christian, and to be willing to let Christ remove whatever held them back. As you read these pages, however different the immediate circumstances in them, I believe you will find incidents that you can relate to, incidents that could tell you something you might need to hear, and to heed.

Like Peter, I learned lessons the hard way. And I've learned sometimes it's best to let God, the divine surgeon, remove what is really holding me back.

Chapter
Ten

PICKING UP THE PIECES

I'M SURPRISED HOW IT HANGS IN my mind, still: vividly, graphically, deeply embedded in my mind. No, it was not the sea of signs and placards and enthusiastic crowds that represent our republic. And it had nothing to do with the headlines and news bulletins.

But it had everything to do with life, and how we live it.

My daughter and I were returning from a marathon of bedside visitation at the hospital. We were in a stream of traffic that had slowed to a crawl, when, on the right side, I saw him. I didn't see what had happened or when it happened. But it was easy to reconstruct what *might have happened.*

From his sweat-stained work clothes, it was evident he was coming home from work. There was a sagging weariness about his body as he bent over in the middle of the street. He was holding an open foam food tray and was carefully schooling back into the container nuggets and potato chunks that had fallen from the container into the street.

In a matter of seconds we were swept up in the traffic and left the scene. But the painful image followed me: a man, bent over—picking up pieces. It staked a claim on my mind and triggered for me a past experience where things had fallen apart and hopes were dumped, and when I was left picking up the pieces.

> When bent over with frustration, disappointment, and anger, we must remember God will always be with us.

I was in Washington the night before a major banquet, where major grants were to be announced. As president of Oakwood College, I was to be a recipient of a million-dollar grant. I even had the letter of confirmation. Then the stunning phone call came, tracking me down at the hotel to let me know the foundation would not be announcing that grant at the banquet this year.

Like the man bent over to pick up his dropped food, I was left trying to scoop up the pieces of plans, pride, and self-esteem.

Have you lived long enough to have something similar happen to you? A crushing blow in life? The real question is how many times has life found you bent over trying to pick up the pieces, the remnants of spilled plans, hopes, relationships, dreams?

Yes, you can remember. Those times are a painful part of living life and leading.

> We are going to get knocked down. The question is:
> How do we respond?

We've all been there personally, professionally, publicly, privately trying to pick up the pieces. You know those times when you try to do your best and things did not turn out the way you intended. Someone helpful said, "One door closes, another opens." And as someone has said, "Yeah, but it's tough out in the hallway."

It happens, and when it does, the fact that you have been knocked down is not the main point. What is the main point is, instead, the length of time you remain down. I always appreciate the perspective of one who put it this way when asked, "Are you ever down?" The answer is, "No, I'm never down. I'm either up or getting up."

We are going to get knocked down. The question is: How do you respond? Do you get angry, bitter, and resentful? Or do you allow them to be scalpel moments as well, moments where you can learn, grow, even help shed the excess baggage of pride, ambition, desire?

It's not often that I've cried in a hotel room. After the tears, I decided to skip the banquet, but I managed to remember another part of the living of life, a truth from this text in the Bible: "I will always be with you. Be strong and of good courage" *(Deuteronomy 31:6)*.

And I have a strategy for living that way too: "Be still, and know that I am God" (Psalm 46:10).

But then I felt a change of heart. I was impressed to go to the banquet. I ended up sitting at table #1 with several top donors, any one of whom could have given a lot of money. In fact, a few years later I did see the grant realized.

That was important, but more important was the fact that, when bent over with frustration, disappointment, and anger, we must remember God's words to us: "I will always be with you" (Deuteronomy 31:6). What a comfort it is to know, there are times when the sky has caved in and the bottom has fallen out and *God is right there picking up the pieces of my life.*

Wait patiently for the Lord.
Be brave and courageous.
Yes, wait patiently for the Lord.
Psalm 27:14, NLT

Yes, He's right there picking up the pieces of my life, if we are surrendered and let Him do that. This might involve some scalpel moments, but like successful surgery, it is certainly worth all that pain that comes before the pieces are put back together, maybe even stronger than they were before.

Chapter
Eleven

"BUT IF NOT" . . .
THE MISSING INGREDIENT

I'VE NOTICED WITH THE PASSAGE of time that there seem to be occurrences that multiply with age. One is the problem of not being able to find a vital item. This can be especially problematic if the item is immediately essential—like car keys when you are already late for an important appointment.

And then, wonder of wonders, in the mail—just what I needed popped up in an advertising brochure from my caring friends at Sharper Image. The brochure cleverly asked if you are always losing your glasses or your remote or your keys. If so, now you can find them. For only

$69.95, you can be the proud owner of a wireless electronic locator. Included with the locator is a generous array of stick-ons to put on each item you need to keep track of. If I can't find that important item, no worry; just get the electronic control and push the button. The missing item will flash and beep.

But my immediate concern is not the Sharper Image catalogue, with its lost item locator, but something far more important than looking for your remote.

As we know, life has its ups and its down. We can go from a mountaintop experience to the valley of pain and suffering and disappointment. It may be that from the high place of one moment you are going into a valley dark with the mysteries of God's dealings with you. You may stumble into a sudden turn and be faced with unexplainable struggles that are the opposite of what you prayed and hoped for.

So my nagging concern at this time is about a missing ingredient, one that can bring peace, comfort, understanding, and perspective to the difficult days of the Christian life.

So, then, where can we find that missing ingredient that impacts victorious living in such a deeply profound way? Strangely enough, in looking for that which can impact the here-and-now of modern life, we must search in the there-and-then of Old Testament life in the book of Daniel. Many consider it difficult to understand the book of Daniel, with its prophecies, symbols, and dates. But couched in those pages, one of the familiar heroic narratives of Holy Scripture looms large with lessons for our lives today.

It was lonely in Babylon. Yes, there were thousands gathered on the plain of Dura, where the king on an ego trip called together VIPs, governors, advisors, treasurers, judges, and magistrates. They all were there—Babylon's high and mighty and the people with power, authority, and influence. They were first standing, then bowing before the solid golden image of himself that King Nebuchadnezzar had set up.

> With any job or calling there are going to be times when your faith will clash with your career.

The Bible expresses it like this: "'To you it is commanded, O peoples, nations, and languages, that at the time you hear the sound of the horn, flute, harp, lyre, and psaltery, in symphony with all kinds of music, you shall fall down and worship the gold image that King Nebuchadnezzar has set up; and whoever does not fall down and worship shall be cast immediately into the midst of a burning fiery furnace.' So at that time, when all the people heard the sound of the horn, flute, harp, and lyre, in symphony with all kinds of music, all the people, nations, and languages fell down and worshiped the gold image which King Nebuchadnezzar had set up" (Daniel 3:4–7).

The mandate was, at the given signal everyone should bow down.

But it was lonely. It's lonely when everyone else is bowing down and you're standing up alone.

What statue of gold has society placed before you to bow down to?

It was true then, and it's true now. Whether you are going against the tide of peer pressure or refusing to do the illegal or unethical at the cost of a good job, it can be lonely. And it was lonely for Shadrach, Meshach, and Abed-nego, three Hebrew captives in Babylon who had just been set over the affairs of nation. Clearly, they were on the fast track, co-winners of the Babylonian Apprentice. But you know, and as they found out, with any job or calling there are going to be times when your faith will clash with your career. It's just a fact of life, a life of faith.

Then the question is: *What statue of gold has society placed before you to bow down before: money, position, power, prestige, popularity, or the creature comforts of a Cadillac culture?*

In addition, the temptation for Daniel and his colleagues to bow down was strengthened by the harsh fact that the punishment for not bowing down to the golden image was to be thrown into a burning fiery furnace.

Talk about consequences.

In addition, it seems that compromise could have been easy. They could have bowed down and justified/rationalized:

"We are only pretending to worship."

"It won't hurt this one time. I'll just go through the motions. When you're in Rome, do as the Romans. In Babylon, as the Babylonians."

"If you want to get along, go along."

No one wants to stick out. And certainly no one wants to be thrown alive into a burning fiery furnace either.

It is always a great temptation to do what everyone else does.

But the three refused to bow and worship the

image of gold. The three refused to compromise, even though everyone else bowed down and worshiped. They drew a line they would not cross, and they remained standing behind it.

> True faith means trusting God and His word, believing without seeing, knowing without feeling.

For some of us, though, our drawing that line is like the playground confrontations where, with the toe of a worn sneaker, we used to draw a line and pronounce, "I dare you to step over that line." And as the adversary stepped over, then we would draw another, all the while threatening, "You better not step over *this* line." Soon, there were lines all across the playground.

Not so the Hebrew boys; they drew the line, then stood alone. Or maybe not as alone as we might think, for look at what happened when, refusing to obey, they were thrown into the flames.

"And these three men, Shadrach, Meshach, and Abed-nego, fell down bound into the midst of the burning fiery furnace. Then King Nebuchadnezzar was astonished; and he rose in haste and spoke, saying to his counselors, 'Did we not cast three men bound into the midst of the fire?' They answered and said to the king, 'True, O king.' 'Look!' he answered, 'I see four men loose, walking in the midst of the fire; and they are not hurt, and the form of the fourth is like the Son of God'" *(Daniel 3:23–25)*.

It was lonely, until company came. And the form of the fourth, in the furnace, looked like the Son of Man. In answer to their prayer for mercy and deliverance, the Lord came down into the furnace to be with them and protect them. And Scripture records the same fire that was to destroy them, set them free from their bonds.

Now, a word of warning: it's easy to get caught up in this gloriously inspiring, marvelously encouraging conclusion. Even the king testified: "There is no other God who can deliver like this" *(Daniel 3:29)*.

But remember—we're looking for that crucial ingredient that for too many of us is the missing ingredient, and finding that takes us back into the heart of the story before that dramatic conclusion.

It's contained in three simple words, almost buried in the flow of the narrative when the king, hearing about their refusal, threatened them. "Shadrach, Meshach, and Abed-nego answered and said to the king, 'O Nebuchadnezzar, we have no need to answer you in this matter. If that is the case, our God whom we serve is able to deliver us from the burning fiery furnace, and He will deliver us from your hand, O king. *But if not*, let it be known to you, O king, that we do not serve your gods, nor will we worship the gold image which you have set up"' *(Daniel 3:16–18).*

There it is, the missing ingredient, found in the phrase *but if not*. A little phrase few in words but huge in its implication. *But if not*. Words that thrill and challenge; words that firmly state conviction that we will remain faithful, despite the consequences. Whether deliverance or death, we will not budge.

It's as if they were saying: "We don't know whether our God will rescue us. He can do it, He is able, but the basis upon which our decision, and our refusal to bow, rests on the idea of *but if not*. He can rescue us, but if He chooses not to, we will not change."

That's a faith that accepts and affirms God has larger meanings in life that we are not able to understand. That God has larger answers to our prayers than we are able to anticipate. That God has a thousand ways of fulfilling His promise in human lives that trust Him. And so whatever the furnace, the trial, the dark valley, if He does not deliver us, our faith is not at an end. If He does not deliver us, our resolution is entirely unshaken. We still believe God, whether we are delivered or not.

'But if not' faith is not faith in deliverance; it is faith in God.

But if not. That's the missing ingredient we must have. For blessed is the man, woman, boy, or girl who goes into the furnaces of life with a faith like this.

Someone is thinking maybe comfortably, if not smugly, "But I have faith." A fair question might be, *What kind of faith do we have?*

Spare tire faith used only in case of emergency? Wheelbarrow faith easily upset and must be pushed? Bus faith, ridden only when it's going our way?

I can hear you protesting, *No, I have faith. I believe with all my heart God will deliver me out of these fearsome circumstances. I have faith God will heal my illness. I have faith God will prolong my days, and faith God will expand my ministry. Faith God will remove the mountains in my path. I believe He can and believe He will.*

Notice, the faith we emphasize and identify with is that our God is able and our God will.

And He certainly is! But I would contend in addition, there must be the *but if not* element as well, a faith that trusts God whether or not the wanted deliverance comes, a faith that bridges the unsettling gap between expectation and experience, a faith that accepts God's will not merely with resignation but with positive enthusiasm.

> Faith is taking the first step even when you don't see the whole staircase.
> Martin Luther King, Jr.

What was demonstrated at Babylon was a *but if not* faith which relates itself not only to the commands of God but to His seeming contradictions. This is not faithlessness. It is faith which says *but if not*, my course is already clear. The decision is made and the matter is settled.

I would insist we all need this missing ingredient, for we all have our furnaces of trial, persecution, unbearable sickness, agonizing loss, unexpected heartbreak, and unrelenting pressure. Yes, furnaces vary, but whatever the furnace, you need the missing ingredient to take you through.

That's why this missing ingredient is so crucial and critical. Like a missing jigsaw piece, it can complete the picture in those days of perplexing experiences that await us all. Without it, our picture and understanding of God is distorted and incomplete and we are left questioning.

Then what we perceive as unanswered prayer in the past wilts our willingness to pray boldly. We get caught judging God on the basis of what we think we should do or what He should have done. We fail to remember that His view of life and His providential perspectives are essentially larger than ours.

You see, when you get down to furnace time, and you will, this thing of trusting God's providence makes a difference in the way we face temptation, trials, tribulations. *But if not* is not blind to the realities of the situation or to the fact that God works out His purposes in the way He chooses, not necessarily in the way we would choose. God does not move on our timetable. And some of His operations don't add up on man-made calculators.

Or, as I've often commented, maybe the little boy wasn't confused when he complained that he didn't understand why God put so many vitamins in spinach and didn't put more of them in ice cream. Maybe he had a revelation that things don't always fit together the way we think.

But if not faith is not faith in deliverance; it is faith in God. Big faith proclaims we are confident of His power, and trust His providence, whatever the furnace contains.

Faith is deliberate confidence in the character of God whose ways you may not understand at the time.
Oswald Chambers

What it boils down to is being able to say: "Lord, I believe that you're able to protect me and my family from all danger and illness. But even if not, I will not bow down and serve the god of bitterness."

It's a faith that says: "God, I believe you are able to preserve my job and reputation if I take a stand for what I believe to be right and just, *but if not* I will not bow down and serve the god of cowardice and go the way of the crowd. Like Lillian Hellman, the noted author and playwright, who stated, "I cannot and will not cut the cloth of my conscience to fit this year's fashion."

It is faith that says: "God, I believe you are able to open the door into that job or ministry that seems right for me to pursue. *But even if not,*

I will not bow down and serve the gods of anxiety and despair."

It is a faith that says: "God, I believe you are able to help me find a life partner and enjoy all the gifts of marriage and family, but *even if not* I will not bow and serve the gods of self-pity, lust, and gratification. I will serve you."

That kind of faith means trusting God and His word, believing without seeing, knowing without feeling. It is a trusting willingness to follow Him, whatever His purpose, whatever the path of His providence.

Like the Hebrew boys, if He delivers us, we will praise Him and continue to trust; and if He doesn't deliver us, we will praise Him and continue to trust Him.

But saying it is one thing; doing it is another. When you settle the trusting of God's providence, then prepare to celebrate God's power manifested in the way His providence determines best for your life and mine and for the larger sweep of God's eternal plan.

As a contemporary gospel poet put it: "I've got confidence God's going to see me through, no matter the way may be; I know he's going to fix it for me."

That kind of conviction is not a spur of the

moment in the heat of battle statement; it is, instead, experience rooted and grounded in the soil of a relationship.

> Though he slay me,
> yet will I trust in him.
> Job 13:15, KJV

Trusting God is first of all a matter of the will. It is my choice and is not dependent on my feelings. But while trusting God is a matter of the will, we must depend upon the Holy Spirit for the enabling power to do it.

This does not mean we do not experience pain. It means we believe that God is at work through the occasion of our pain for our ultimate good.

The noted preacher Fred Craddock tells of some early teens reciting Scriptures memorized before the congregation. It was to show what they had learned from parts of Romans 8. The teacher started with the first boy at the front of the line.

"George, what shall separate you from the love of God?"

George answered: "I am persuaded that neither death nor life," and he finished with a smile. As his parents smiled, the teacher went next to Mary.

"Mary, what can separate you from love of God."

She recited the verses from Romans 8.

As the teacher moved down the line, the congregation grew anxious because at the end of the line was Rachel, a sweet child of warm smile and easy grace, a Down syndrome child. The fear of onlookers was wondering if she could really memorize Romans 8. The question moved closer until, "Rachel, what can separate you from the love of God?"

Rachel flashed that familiar smile, and then she said one word, "Nothing!"

Nothing.

"And I am convinced that *nothing* can ever separate us from God's love. Neither death nor life, neither angels nor demons, neither our fears for today nor our worries about tomorrow—not even the powers of hell can separate us from God's love. No power in the sky above or in the earth below— indeed, nothing in all creation will ever be able to separate us from the love of God that is revealed in Christ Jesus our Lord" *(Romans 8:38–39, NLT).*

Chapter Twelve

No One is Disposable

ACTUALLY, TRUTH BE TOLD, I was proud of my idea. I feel I'm a practical and pragmatic person who leans toward what works and what is the quickest. Time is to be maximized.

One example of that was when I became president of Oakwood College. The answering message I placed on my home telephone machine was, "Speak." No long eloquent apology about missing the call and so forth. Just "Speak."

I got that idea from a fire department phone whose greeting message was one word, "Address." Obviously with my "get on with it" mentality, it should have been no surprise that

I introduced a radical concept of Thanksgiving dinner protocol.

I had long been a proponent of convenience. So I told my wife (I mean I *suggested* to my wife) that I would handle the table for Thanksgiving. And I planned to do it with an all-paper/plastic spread: plates, forks, cups, napkins, tablecloth, etc. Everything that could be was paper/plastic. My finest moment came when dinner was over and I expeditiously picked up the corners of the paper tablecloth and bundled up the whole shebang and dropped it into a Hefty trash bag.

Voila! Done! Really done, because my loving wife declared it was done and would be done no more.

It worked for one reason, though: everything was disposable.

Unfortunately, we are living in a disposable society—a throwaway society. For the most part we love it. It makes life easier. We use disposable diapers, plates, and soda pop cans. Vacationers can snap pictures with disposable cameras. We now even have disposable wedding gowns!

But to our chagrin we are discovering that the throwing-away habit we love so much comes with a price. It comes with risks. It is an ominous peril. Our habits are not just polluting our seas but destroying our land, the air we breathe, and all kinds of wildlife.

But there is another peril that lurks in our throwaway society—a more subtle problem, but far more dangerous. Alvin Toffler over fifteen years ago warned us about it in his now-famous book *Future Shock*. We are living in a disposable society with *disposable people*. We are living in a society where it seems beliefs about human dignity and human worth are not slowly being eroded, but rapidly being washed away.

> We need to
> see people as
> Jesus saw them.

We see it in the news every day: ruthless gang shootings and senseless freeway killings. We have read about a newborn baby who was abandoned in the trash can. Another baby was left on the steps of a local church.

Our relationships with people, places, and things in our throwaway society are utilitarian, temporary, and disposable. The average American moves every five years. We change jobs. We are unable to develop long-term relationships. People become disposable. But the reason I bring all this up is because we need a corrective to this mentality.

We need to see people as Jesus saw them.

"A certain man was there who had an illness for thirty-eight years" *(John 5:5, MEV)*. Jesus saw him lying there, and He knew the man had been sick for a long time. For it was there at the pool that Jesus approached him, to ask about the one thing the man felt he wanted above everything else. For at the pool, Jesus asked that innocent, reasonable question, "Do you want to be made well?" *(John 5:6)*.

> Jesus saw the great potential
> in Peter and wasn't going to
> let it be thrown away.

It was a rhetorical question. Of course he did. But Jesus wanted him to be made well. Jesus saw him, not just as he was, but what he could be. He saw the potential there, waiting to be brought out. He was not a disposable thing; he was a human being, and thus Jesus healed him.

We can see this with the story of Simon Peter. Jesus told him that though he was called Simon, his name would now be Peter, and "Peter" from the Greek means "rock." What Jesus was saying to him was: "Peter, I know you. I know what men say about you. I know that you are a profane pretender. I know that you're a blustering braggart. I know that you're vacillating. I know that you're weak. I know that you're unstable. I know that you are a coward, but you shall be. You shall be. I see a Peter whose loyalty will be unlimited. You shall be. You shall be."

That is, He saw the great potential in Peter and wasn't going to let it be thrown away.

My personal reaction to the TV show *Cops* is negative. It shows people at their worst. I deeply feel as Samuel Dewitt Proctor put it: "Everybody is God's somebody." We are called to be in community, to be in fellowship with God and with each other. We can't go it alone. We have to be together.

To Jesus, no one is disposable. Not even me, not even you.

No one is disposable. No throwaways, no *disposable* human beings. It's this perception of relationships and people as disposable that Jesus and the Word of God absolutely reject today.

Look to the example of Jesus. See Him touching the leper—the clear outcast of society. See Him healing the blind, casting out demons. See Him giving food to the poor, preaching hope to the discouraged, eating meals with sinners. To Jesus, no one is disposable.

Not even me, not even you. That's how in love He sees us . . . perceptively, positively, and patiently. It was summed up in a little cartoon I received some time ago that said: "If God had a refrigerator, your picture would be on it."

Chapter
Thirteen

SALT

FROM THE SLOPE OF THE gentle rise of the unnamed mount next to Lake Gennesaret, the Master's words, now known as the Sermon on the Mount, roll down through the years and across the broad sweep of the landscape of life and even onto the words that are before your eyes now, here in the twenty-first century.

Jesus had spent the night seeking divine guidance. Following that night of prayer He then called His twelve disciples. So the Sermon on the Mount was actually delivered to the twelve, although the ever-present multitude heard it as well. The Master's words were not general, but specific to aspects of the kingdom life that would characterize His disciples.

And, in a modern paraphrase, His words read like this: "You're blessed when you're at the end of your rope. With less of you there is more of God. Blessed when you feel you've lost what is most dear to you." Revolutionary concepts. "Count yourself blessed every time people put you down or . . . speak lies about you . . . Give a cheer!" *(Matthew 5:11–12, MSG).*

Of 100 unsaved men,
one might read the Bible,
but the other 99 will
read the Christian.

Jefferson Bethke

These were ideas that were foreign to the understanding of the world then, and to the world now. At the conclusion of this marvelous listing, Jesus uses a significant metaphor to describe the nature and characteristics of His followers. "You are the salt of the earth" *(Matthew 5:13).*

Quite frankly it was a startling announcement that might seem to border on arrogance. Remember whom He was speaking to. They were unlearned, unlettered, untried, unknown.

They were just beginning their journey following the Master. What had they demonstrated to be worthy of that designation?

After all, salt of the earth was no mean title. Salt was greatly valued, as precious as human life. Salt of great value was used as barter. Part of a Roman soldier's pay was given to him in salt. It was called a *salarium*, and from this word comes our word "salary."

Salt of the earth was, then, a title of privilege. And yet, with amazing confidence, Jesus told these spiritual and theological neophytes, "You are the salt of the earth"?

It was, and it is, a profound pronouncement of privilege, though as it is used here it does not fit the current society's view of privilege. It's like the view of the wealthy lady arriving at a five-star hotel and ordering the bellman to carry her son into the hotel. The bellman, in disbelief, exclaimed, "Lady, he's big enough to walk!" To which she responded, "Isn't it precious that he doesn't have to." That view of privilege comes with the notion of avoiding responsibilities, of avoiding having to do things others have to do. Like waiting to board the airplane while others go first, we prize our frequent flyer early boarding privileges and our airline club privileges.

In many ways our society wants privilege without responsibility, delights without the duties, crown without the cross, and pay without performance.

That is not what Jesus is saying here. Privilege is inextricably linked with responsibility. No advantages of discipleship without the responsibilities of discipleship. "You are the salt of the earth."

In these few verses, powerful, challenging truths travel here, first of all.

The profound privilege, "You are." Understanding the crucial nature, the enormous value of salt, in a few words Jesus reminds them and us. The world is in need of the salt of the Christian life.

> People may hear your words, but they feel your attitude.
> John C. Maxwell

There are needs all around us—some we are clearly aware of, while others we may miss. Like the dad pushing a shopping cart down the aisle in the grocery store with a red-faced, screaming child. The father repeats, "Easy, Freddy; calm down, Freddy; come on, don't get upset." When a woman shopper passes by and coos, "You're very patient with Freddy," his quick response is, "Lady, I'm Freddy!"

Jesus reminds us that needs all around us are met by divine provision. To these untried, unproven, unpromising disciples you are not yet what you will learn to be. No, you are salt because of divine initiative, not because of anything in yourself.

> The kingdom life is an inner condition resulting in outward attitudes and aptitudes.

His emphasis underscores the kingdom life as an inner condition resulting in outward attitudes and aptitudes. It views the Christian character not as something to possess, but as being and doing. It is an active, not a passive, verb.

Yet it also must be salt. No extraordinary, headline-grabbing exploits. Instead, silently, with consistency and dependability in a day-to-day witness. In words sometimes attributed to Francis of Assisi—"Preach the gospel all the time. If necessary, use words."[4]

Look at what came before the salt metaphor:

"Blessed are the poor in spirit,
For theirs is the kingdom of heaven.
Blessed are those who mourn,
For they shall be comforted.
Blessed are the meek,
For they shall inherit the earth.
Blessed are those who hunger and
    thirst for righteousness,
For they shall be filled.
Blessed are the merciful,
For they shall obtain mercy.
Blessed are the pure in heart,
For they shall see God.
Blessed are the peacemakers,
For they shall be called sons of God.
Blessed are those who are persecuted
    for righteousness' sake,
For theirs is the kingdom of heaven.
"Blessed are you when they revile and persecute you, and say all kinds of evil against you falsely for My sake. Rejoice and be exceedingly glad, for great is your reward in heaven, for so they persecuted the prophets who were before you. You are the salt of the earth; but if the salt loses its flavor, how shall it be seasoned? It is then good for nothing but to be thrown out and trampled underfoot by men" *(Matthew 5:3–13)*.

The words about salt were an apt conclusion to that which has gone before. Jesus is saying that those who give expression to the gentle, the humble, the sensitive, the caring, the hopeful—these are the persons who make the difference in the world, the kind of difference salt makes. The difference Christians are to make in society.

Salt must be in contact to be effective.

If you know the Bible, you know that Jesus sent them as He sends us into the world. The salt was not to just sit. It was to go and be an influence on all it came into contact with. Salt must be in contact to be effective. In every area of life, especially at home and at work, it must be seen. The late news anchor Peter Jennings underscored that in a probing *Primetime* documentary highlighting the growing tide of people taking God into the workplace, integrating spiritual life and work life.

The fact is we spend more than half of our waking hours at work. The Christian life cannot be lived outside, excluding the workplace. We are to be salt at home and at work.

Yes, even at work. I know, work is about being

competitive, hard-nosed toughness, competition. Business is business. Jesus doesn't fit in with deadlines and bottom lines.

But our cue should be that Jesus used images and the language of working life: sheep, shepherds, workers, vineyards, fisherman, and day laborers. Scripture reports that Jesus spoke to the employers and employees of His time— landowners, tenant farmers, merchants, soldiers, tax collectors, shepherds.

In no way did His teaching escape the working world. The cog began right in the midst of human life. We are the salt of the earth, so our faith is not private and ornamental. We must affect our involvement with others in the community.

"Salt must be mingled with the substance to which it is added; it must penetrate and infuse . . . so it is through personal contact and association that men are reached by the saving power of the gospel." [5]

Being salt has everything to do with it penetrating the everyday life of the world with its distinctive alternative rather than with shouting at the world from a distance.

As John Stott puts it, "God intends us to penetrate the world. Christian salt has no business to remain snugly in elegant little ecclesiastical salt containers. Our place is to be rubbed into the secular community."[6]

The privilege is enormous, a marvelous certainty. "You are," an action of grace. However, the scripture goes on.

"You are the salt of the earth; but if the salt loses its flavor, how shall it be seasoned?" Yes, you are the salt of the earth, but He doesn't end it there. "But if the salt . . ." The "but" there is a conjunction with a difference. "And" is likewise a conjunction, but it does not carry the same impact as "but." To say "and" is to give additional information that doesn't change the intent of the statement. In contrast, "but" not only adds additional information but also qualifies that which has gone before.

> The Christian life is a stewardship of character to be developed and used.

While the privilege is a marvelous certainty, "You are the salt of the earth," the peril is a dangerous possibility we must not forget the "but" that follows. Yes, you have been given a great privilege, but with that privilege comes great responsibility.

Don't forget it!

The Christian life is a life lived in the grace of God. But the Christian life is more than a gift of grace. It is a stewardship of character to be developed and used. It calls for divine initiative consciously developing patterns of real thinking.

Unlike that was the observation raised in a conversation in an exclusive corporate club room where one member shared with another, "Look at Johnson sitting over there. He is really thinking." To which the other member quipped, "Johnson thinks he is thinking, but he is merely rearranging his prejudices."

> Our role in society is not to be against it so much as it is to purify or enrich the social order.

Faith calls for real thinking, decision making, and action based on a personal experience with Jesus. Salt is living the gospel on the job. Jesus made it clear for us and for them. We must live out the gospel in our working lives.

I love the way The Message Bible version paraphrase puts it: "Let me tell you why you're here. You're here to be salt-seasoning that brings out the God-flavors of this earth. If you lose your saltiness, how will people taste Godliness?" *(Matthew 5:13, MSG).*

Salt must remain salty.

Our role in society is not to be against it so much as it is to purify or enrich the social order. So, for salt to make a difference, it must not only be in contact, it must not be contaminated, adulterated, or compromised by what it comes in contact with.

As the Clear Word paraphrase renders the verse, "If you hold on to these values, you will be the salt of the earth." We must heed the warning: when the values and virtue are lost, the salt is of no value.

The Christian life, then, means not selling out to the bankrupt values that too often prevail in the world. It does mean a distinctive, unburied lifestyle dispersed in the world rather than remaining physically and psychologically secluded in a religious fortress. The salt metaphor makes it clear there is a fundamental difference between the values of the kingdom and of this secular society. As John Stott puts it: "They are as different as chalk from cheese . . . we serve neither God, nor ourselves, nor the world by attempting to obliterate or minimize this difference." [7]

Be salt to live in the love and manner of Jesus. Take the holy place to the marketplace.

And Jesus is also making it clear that activity without the spiritual relationship is useless. Don't misunderstand this point here. It is possible to look like salt, to be called salt, and yet it is all an illusion.

"How careful then we should be to follow the example of Christ in our lifework. Unless we do this, we are worthless to the world—salt which has lost its savor."[8]

"Jesus used salt as an illustration of the Christian's life and teachings upon the world . . . But if Christians are only so in name . . . they are like the salt that has lost its savor. Their influence upon the world is bad."[9]

Our profession of faith may proclaim the theory of religion, but it is our practical piety that holds forth the word of truth. The consistent life, the holy conversation, the unswerving integrity, the active benevolent spirit, the godly example—this gives salt its power.

There is no middle ground here. Salt is to make a difference. The usefulness, the value of salt is contingent on savor, dispersion, and application. If saltiness and savor are not there, then only grimness is instead. You've lost your usefulness and will end up in the garbage heap.

The key to it all is a relationship with Jesus. Being truly salt cannot be done without the relationship. This truth carries through in all the New Testament. Jesus's ethical teaching in the Sermon on the Mount was preceded by the beatitudes, which reminded Jesus's disciples that God's grace comes before His commands.

Let your light shine before others, that they may see your good deeds and glorify your Father in heaven.

Matt. 5:16, NIV

Being salt starts with being with Him, not just being out there. And being salt continues with being with Him, not just busy out there, but being out there with Him first and foremost in all that we say and do.

That's truly being salt.

Chapter Fourteen

THE ONE WORD, "THEREFORE"

MY NAME IS BENJAMIN Reaves. But each day I am just one postage stamp away from being called Benny Buffett. You see, day after day I get the notifications that I have already won the sweepstakes. The letters come to me personally addressed and they claim that, if I will only mail the form back in, the fact that I'm already a winner will be confirmed by my being a winner.

Have to think about that logic a bit, though . . .

Of course, it's equally intriguing and

deceptive as you watch television and you see the ads and the spots promoting these sweepstakes, and you see real people winning millions of dollars. I've noticed that the most common response or remark seems to be: "I can't believe it! I can't believe it!"

Why such a common response?

Is it because we have been conditioned to expect the ordinary, the routine? The possibility of some extremely good thing happening to us seems to be so remote that, when it does happen—we can't believe it.

> The book of Ephesians affirms that all of us have "hit the jackpot."

Now, what appears to be true in the material realm also seems true in the spiritual realm. Can it be that many of us have trouble believing in the extravagant goodness of God toward us personally? The idea that God would lavish magnificent blessings on us is something we find hard to believe. We find it easier to think of ourselves as unworthy, not good enough, not holy enough or sincere enough to get the really good things from God.

Someone said in a striking way that we have a million-dollar salvation and a five-cent response. The fact remains, and the book of Ephesians affirms, that all of us, in a sense, have "hit the jackpot." And that is because we all have a rich and extravagant inheritance in Christ. And yet, as the Scripture tells us just how rich that inheritance is, we easily find ourselves saying in word or in action: *I can't believe it, I can't believe it.*

But it is true. That is one of the main themes of the book of Ephesians, a book that has been called the Alps of the New Testament or the Queen of the Epistles, as it casts a radiant light and reveals to us the extreme magnitude of God's blessings to us in Christ. Paradoxically, this testimony of God's blessings was written by Paul while he was in prison, serving hard time for his faith, and yet he tells us that we have been given every spiritual blessing—chosen, adopted, accepted, redeemed, forgiven, sealed, guaranteed.

The first three chapters of Ephesians tell us that we are now citizens of a new kingdom and members of a new family. In those chapters we can see what Christ has done for us; we can see our privileged position in Him. We can see the biblical basis of who we are and whose we are.

Then in the remaining chapters, the call

comes to the consequential dimension, and that is to live according to who we are and whose we are.

> We have a million-dollar salvation and a five-cent response.

"I, therefore, the prisoner of the Lord, beseech you to walk worthy of the calling with which you were called, with all lowliness and gentleness, with longsuffering, bearing with one another in love, endeavoring to keep the unity of the Spirit in the bond of peace" *(Ephesians 4:1–3).*

To me, this sounds like challengingly powerful stuff. Yet his words here are not going to be found in the section of the best-selling business books on Amazon. And how do they fit in the high-powered, stress-filled world of healthcare? Sure, this is good material for a sermon, but what does this have to do with being competitive, hard-nosed, aggressive, tough, as one needs to be in this business?

Come on now, really, do these words fit in with deadlines and bottom lines? I mean, check out the ad for Adventist Health System employees. *Here's the kind of folk we are looking for: humble, gentle, patient, loving, peaceful.* Is that what we say? I don't think so.

The fact is these virtues sound less like the workplace and more like Disneyland. I mean, pardon me and my skepticism, but the humanity in me and the humanity I see around me forces out an incredulous, "You've got to be kidding." It could even raise a pragmatic question that cannot be resisted, and that is: *Well, will it work?* I mean it sounds good, makes for good conversation. *But will it work?*

Yet, frankly, that's not the issue. The issue is not one of working, but one of expectation and obligation. For Paul is using one of his favorite metaphors, and he speaks of balance between profession and practice, between calling and character, in actuality, not just in appearance.

Paul would be kidding, except for that single word that appears early in the first verse of Ephesians 4: "therefore." The word "therefore" is a connective, a transitional word indicating Paul is basing all that he states now on the preceding three chapters. While in the first half of the book, Paul explains the riches of God's grace, in the last half of the book, following "therefore," he highlights the responsibilities of the recipients of God's grace. Against the backdrop of God's grace, he says, as another version puts it: "In the light of, therefore."

So our walk is to be a "therefore" walk, a "therefore" goodness, a "therefore" unity. Of course, the nature of membership in any organization is that the aims and objectives of the group become the aims and objectives of the individual. Citizens have an obligation to abide by the laws of their country. Employees likewise are obligated to promote the purposes and goals of the company.

> The message of Ephesians is that in this new society, the church, the highest principle of respect and unity holds true.

At its worst, unfortunately and negatively, on an athletic team, members are required to play as the coach directs. Maybe you have heard of the ridiculous stories about the baseball pitcher sent from the Major Leagues down to the Minor Leagues because he wouldn't intentionally hit the opposing batter; or even worse the Spanish coach motivating his player with racial slurs about the opposing player from France.

But the message of Ephesians is that in this new society, which Christ called into existence in the church, the highest principle of respect and unity holds true. We are citizens of a new kingdom and members of a new family, and the obligations and requirements of this new society come along with the privilege of being a part of it.

It goes with the territory.

Ever hear of the word "d'Artagnan"? D'Artagnan was one of the three musketeers of Alexandre Dumas's work entitled *The Three Musketeers*. The heroes of that story had as their motto, *All for one, and one for all*. This meant that they were vowing to stand together in their common fight.

And I think that Paul, in this epistle, is trying to get the Ephesian church to adopt as their motto: All for one, and one for all. The key to it all is made up of the two words: "in Christ."

But let me begin with a story recounted by Doug Rumfeld, who tells us that the Paris Opera House sits on three acres of land. Most of the theater, about four-fifths, is backstage. There's a subterranean lake that goes seven stories *beneath* the building, and it is an essential part of the structural design. With the water level being raised or lowered, it can support the varying weight of massive sets and different scenes onstage.

How like the reservoir of the soul, the soul that is "in Christ," the One who supports the fluctuating weights and stresses that strain the stage of our daily lives. Ephesians reminds us the backstage design therefore ensures the onstage success.

Abide in me, and I in you.
As the branch cannot bear
fruit by itself, unless it abides
in the vine, neither can you,
unless you abide in me.

John 15:4, ESV

In short, the message, and my message, is this: Live a life worthy of the calling you have received, for that calling is worth more than any sweepstakes you might win here.

Chapter Fifteen

A VITAMIN FOR THE JOURNEY

THE OTHER DAY I WAS reminded that some nameless philosopher commented, "If Mother Nature doesn't get you, Father Time will." Now, of course, the substance of that philosophical statement is that the passage of time affects us all. No question about it. In fact, if I had any doubts about it, I was reminded of that not too long ago.

I was in Washington for meetings and stopped by a supermarket to make some purchases. I was standing in the aisle, trying to decide which way to go, and evidently one of the workers in the store came up in back of me because I heard someone say, "Excuse me, Pops." Well, I looked around to see who "Pops" was and, to my surprise and consternation—I was Pops.

If that weren't enough, my wife and I had just moved to Orlando and we had gone to the supermarket. We purchased our groceries, and I wheeled them out to the car, unloaded them, and, in my cooperative manner, I was wheeling the cart back to the store. As I approached the store, a gentleman came out. Evidently, he was the person that supervised the carts.

As I rolled it up to him, he said, "Why, thank you so much."

"That's quite all right," I replied.

As I turned to go, he said, "Would you like a job"? He followed that up by saying, "You know, if you are retired you can work part time, choose your own hours."

"Well," I answered, "let me think about it, you never know."

You never know, do you?

Time affects us all. Another way I've noticed the passing of time is that you tend to find yourself browsing in unexplored places, such as among the vitamins and the food supplements. The other day, I just happened to be in the drugstore, and just happened to walk through that side of the drugstore where they had certain items, and I noticed the proliferation of vitamins. Specialized vitamins. Vitamins for aging. Vitamins for gray hair. Vitamins for brain power. Vitamins for the heart. Vitamins for the skin. Vitamins for stress. Vitamins for the eyes. Vitamins for whatever you need.

And it occurred to me, as I look across the landscape of life, that what we need is what I call "a vitamin for the journey."

At all times and in all places the eternal God is your refuge.

Now, before going further, this vitamin is not found in the supplement section of Big B or Walgreens. This vitamin cannot be found in the advice of well-known and well-paid media pundits and prophets. In fact, this vitamin is not even found on the psychic hotline. Paradoxically, this vitamin for the journey is found in the last words of a dying man, Moses, who said in his final blessing on the nation of Israel:

"The eternal God is your refuge, and underneath are the everlasting arms" *(Deuteronomy 33:27).*

Here we see Moses's last will and testament

and, most definitely, his final testimony. These blessings carried the authority of God and, as such, provided encouragement, assurance, and strength for the journey.

God is our
refuge and strength;
a very present
help in trouble.
Ps. 46:1, ESV

Fine, but still, why this text as "the vitamin for the journey"?

Because of the first phrase of the text, which says: "The eternal God is your refuge." Now immediately certain words stand out in the verse. First of all, the word for God there is in the plural, standing as it does for the immeasurable might and majesty of the Most High.

And then you look quickly and there is another arresting word in the text. It's the word that's translated "eternal." Now eternal, as it is used here, does not mean the same as "everlasting." The word translated "eternal" here has another meaning or nuance and it has to do also with yesterday. And so the thought of the verse could be translated: *The eternal God, the God of the beginning, the God who existed from the eternal past, this God of old is our dwelling place and our refuge.*

But another word that comes to our attention is the word "refuge." Now that's a word that has a powerful attraction, and that's because millions of dollars are spent by men and women trying to find a refuge.

In fact, do you know that this large annual meeting sometimes called camp meeting is a refuge? Don't take camp meeting for granted. For many people, camp meeting is the opportunity for fellowship and the association with those of like faith; but for many people this is not an optional arrangement but an absolute necessity for survival.

It is a refuge.

Then, of course, those who may not have lots of money to spend turn to the television to try to find their getaway with the rich and the famous. The point is, people are always looking for a refuge.

But as we all know: you can't put miles between yourself and pain; can't put miles between yourself and difficulty; can't put miles between yourself and sorrow.

Moses knew that. He saw the need for refuge, and not just any old refuge but refuge found only in the eternal God—the God who brought him out of Egypt, out of bondage and slavery.

The God, who is no Johnny-come-lately, is the same God who called Abraham and blessed Jacob and kept Isaac and met Moses in the burning bush. This God, the only God, the eternal God—He is your refuge.

The passage is clear that, under all circumstances and difficulties, God is your refuge. Whether it is the raging tempest or the daily drizzle, whether it's minor grief or major hurts—at all times and in all places the eternal God is my refuge.

> If there is something,
> anything, that gets
> between you and God,
> then whatever it is—
> it needs a scalpel moment.

Now what that means to me is that when the rat race is frantic and I can't measure up to keeping up—the eternal God is my refuge. When you are terrified, panicked, just plain scared, and you can no longer hide it—the eternal God is your refuge. When you are tired, tired of being tired, and you need rest for your body and your soul—the eternal God is your refuge.

Some people right now might not feel the need for refuge; things, right now, might be going rather nicely for them. But believe me, there are people right now who know life has a way of shaking their soul to its foundation. The time will come when you will need to know not only that you have a refuge, but that that refuge is the eternal God, and you can't let anything get in your way of coming to that refuge.

If there is something, anything, that gets between you and God, then whatever it is—it needs a scalpel moment.

Several years ago, a submarine was being tested; as part of the test, the sub had to remain submerged for a number of hours.

When it finally returned back to the harbor, the engineers asked the captain: "Hey, how did you fare in the terrible storm?"

"What storm?" he asked. "We didn't even know there was a storm."

Of course—the submarine had been so far beneath the surface that it had reached that area known to sailors as "the cushion of the sea," so although the ocean may be whipped into huge waves by high winds on the surface, the waters below are never stirred.

The lesson is obvious. The eternal God is "your cushion of the sea." And there, sheltered by His grace, you can find, even in the storm, the tranquility that only God can provide.

God is our refuge from the storm. When it seems as if everything nailed down is breaking loose, or the sky is caving in and the bottom is falling out, we must place ourselves underneath the everlasting arms.

Surely, then, this passage in Deuteronomy is a vitamin for the journey. For in the first place, the eternal God is your refuge. That is reason enough, but this idea prepares and leads us to the second part of the declaration, which is: we are underneath the everlasting arms.

> No matter how far down you have been, you have never been lower than those everlasting arms.

In Scripture, arms always constitute the figure of strength. And the everlasting arms emphasize the continuing power and majesty of God's arms. Everlasting arms is another way of describing the help that God offers, the help that comes as we need it.

I love the story of little Susie, who, in her prayers, was going down her little checklist. She said: "Dear God, before I finish, remember, God, I want you to take care of Mommy, take care of Daddy, uh yeah, take care of my brother, and please, God, take care of yourself because if you don't, we are all sunk. Amen."

Underneath the everlasting arms. Interestingly enough, the Hebrew word for "underneath" means "the bottom." The root word is that of pressing the very bottom as far down as can be. So the question is, *How far down can your imagination take you?* (Or is that the place you don't want to go, even if only in your imagination?)

On the other hand, how far down has your experience taken you? How far down has the crushing weight of sorrow taken you? How far down have you fallen in some hour of weakness?

What this passage is saying is that no matter how far down you have been, no matter how far you have fallen, whatever the lowest level you've ever known—you have never been lower than those everlasting arms, which are always below you, at the bottom, to catch you before you reach it. Underneath all grief, all loneliness, all pain, all weakness—the everlasting arms are there.

That's where many of us have found the truth

of the everlasting arms as we've never known them before. It was in a moment of weakness, when we had gone down as far as we thought we could go.

Such as what happened with Harry Saulnier, the former superintendent of the popular Christian radio program known as Pacific Garden Mission. He told how, before his conversion, he had been a lifelong drunkard, and then he confessed how, at the funeral of his baby daughter, he took the white burial shoes off her feet and sold them for a drink.

Underneath *even that* were the everlasting arms of a loving God.

I don't know the full story of this man, but I have no doubt to get from where he had been to where he went, he certainty had his scalpel moment. In fact, if we could ask him, he would surely say that *he had plenty of them*. But he can thank God that He was there, even when he was that low, in order to do the needed cutting!

God is our refuge?

Ask an adulterer, David. Ask a profane Peter. Ask a violent Paul. All these could testify to the fact that no matter how far down you go, God is there to meet, to catch you, and to bring you back.

"The eternal God is your refuge, and underneath are the everlasting arms" *(Deuteronomy 33:27)*.

This is your personal prescription because God wants a personal encounter with you. This prescription has your name written on it.

God is calling your name. He wants a personal encounter for you. This is a personal prescription for a vitamin for the journey. This is a miracle vitamin. It can heal ulcers. This vitamin can remove wrinkles—the wrinkles of worry. This vitamin can lower blood pressure. This vitamin can strengthen the weak muscles of your will. This vitamin can calm your jittery nerves. This vitamin can enhance your quality of sleep. This vitamin can build your moral endurance.

> In Jesus dwells all the fullness of the Godhead. He is all that we have, all that we need.

But understand—this vitamin is not a supplement. This vitamin is your sufficiency because He is your all in all. He was before all things, and by Him all things consist. In Him dwells all the fullness of the Godhead. He is all that we have, all that we need.

Chapter
Sixteen

LIVING EXPECTANTLY

I'M SURE THAT YOU HEAR IT sometimes on the elevator. At other times, if you're waiting in a doctor's office you hear it. If you're shopping in the mall, you hear it. More and more, in different ways and in different places, you hear sounds, rhythms, melodies, and songs of yesterday, the "golden oldies." These songs and their frequent occurrence are the result of a profitable area of the music industry. The nostalgia craze is where specialized stations are devoted to playing what they call "the songs of your life." The fascinating thing about it is that these stations capitalize on a hunger for nostalgia. They wrap precious memories in melodies and phrases of the old songs.

But it is interesting that this modern mania for nostalgia is confronted and challenged by a Scripture: "Remember ye not the former things, neither consider the things of old" *(Isaiah 43:18, KJV)*. Or, as another version puts it: "Forget the former things; do not dwell on the past" (NIV).

At first glance, this passage appears to be a contradiction. For in the early part of the chapter, Israel has been reminded of its history. Then, as the chapter proceeds in verse 18, Israel is called to: "Remember ye not the former things, neither consider the things of old."

Is this really a contradiction, or perhaps what verse 18 really means is that Israel must refuse to be prisoners of a *negative* past? That is, Israel is being called to forget the failures, the disappointments, the guilt, the shame, and the hypocrisy of its previous history.

There's no question that Israel had a past to forget. Israel had a sad past, a checkered past, so it appears logical that what this passage is saying is that Israel must forget it and, instead, press on ahead to the future.

If that is what the Scripture is saying, then there's a message here for us: let's forget the pain and the disappointments and the problems of the past. This idea, no doubt, has a strong attraction for those of us who still live in haunted houses—houses haunted by the ghosts of painful memories. You know, memories that barely cover unhealed wounds. Or, if they have healed, they're covered with the painful growth of scar tissue.

"For I know the plans I have for you," says the Lord. "They are plans for good and not for disaster, to give you a future and a hope."
Jer. 29:11, NLT

Who doesn't have memories of some difficult situations? Memories of some miserable failures, of times that we would rather forget. Memories of a time of shame, when you could hear in your mind the words of condemnation, "How are the mighty fallen!" Perhaps the memories of those painfully negative statements when you were told that you would never amount to anything, and perhaps memories of the times when you seemed to be living proof of those predictions that you would never amount to anything? That past has almost become a reality for you, to the point where you're tempted to give up on yourself. If the text is suggesting that we should not be prisoners of a negative past, then in many ways, and in many hearts, we would welcome that understanding.

But that's not quite the emphasis of the passage because in some verses before, the Lord talked about how He had delivered them from Babylon; that is, the Lord was pointing them to their past and the tragedies of it. The text then talks about the One who made a way in the sea, a path through the waters for them to escape, despite all their mistakes and failures.

Thus, it appears that what the chapter is saying here is that what is to be remembered no more are the mighty acts and works of God.

Is that what it is saying? If so, that's strange and certainly contradicts a lot of other Bible texts that talk about remembering the great works of God. Or, perhaps the emphasis in the passage is not that Israel should refuse to be prisoners of a negative past, but that Israel must not be prisoners of a *positive past*?

What does that mean?

God performed great miracles for Israel. But the problem was Israel was now living on past blessings. They were locked in the prison of the past. They were locked in a hide-bound faith that looked only *back* on what God had done.

Hence, they ceased to look forward to what God could do. They now had a faith that ceased to expect anything from God. Theirs was a faith that was locked in by memory, and limited by memory.

God's plans for your
life far exceed the
circumstances of your day.
Louie Giglio

Would God's modern spiritual Israel be no different? Could we have for too long lived in the glow of past blessings? I think so. I think that for too long we've subsisted on the crumbs of spiritual nostalgia. When we talk about the power of God in our lives, we're always looking back to that day, back to that time, back to those events and blessings that are part of a positive past that have made us prisoners of the past. I believe that if the only thoughts I can muster up about the power of God and the power of the Spirit relate only to some past pulpit experience of mine, then I am a pulpit has-been, living in the glow of some perceived, past glory, prisoner of a positive past.

It's painful to realize that maybe the blessings of the past set the standard for your expectation of the future. It's painful that, in many marriages, the only hope that there is, the only residue that still exists, is a looking back to the way it was, looking back to the days of courtship, looking back to the early days of marriage. Now husband and wife sit night after night before a television screen, where actors simulate more love and passion than this real couple experience in their marriage now. And so they look back and wish, "Oh, if it could only be like that again!" They are prisoners of a positive past.

It's like that even in sports. For the athlete whose reflexes are gone, whose legs are gone, who lives now to talk about what used to be.

It's, unfortunately, most tragically like that in our spiritual life, where the measure of our expectation is tied to what used to be. We look back to the time when our hearts were once tender to the Gospel's touch, to the time when our enthusiasm was once ablaze, when our commitment to purity and honesty was deep and strong. We look back to the past, to the way it used to be.

It was the longing that could be heard in her voice as she sat in the office and she began to recount what was an astounding description of shame and sordidness. And somehow, in a childish way, she pressed her hands against her face as if somehow that could hold back the tears, but the tears came down around and through her fingers and wrists. And what she said was, "I know God doesn't want to have anything more to do with me."

I don't forget the past, but in the power of Almighty God, I look to a future that will transcend the past.

Her expression is not a painful record of an experience to be read about. The truth is there is an experience that can be enjoyed, and that's what I tried to get across to her as she sat there in the office. I said, "You mean you don't qualify?"

She said, "Yeah, I don't qualify."

And I said, "Oh, yes you do. Your need is your qualification. Whatever your problem. Whatever your past. Whatever your failure. Whatever your need. When we are confronted, intimidated by our hopelessness and helplessness, we can come to Jesus and He will in no wise cast us out."

The fact is that the passage, "Remember ye not the former things," will not let you settle for being a prisoner of a negative past; nor will it let you settle for being a prisoner of a positive past.

The truth is this passage is calling us to a faith that will not be limited by the past. It's calling us to live expectantly. Following verse 18, which says, "Remember ye not the former things," verse 19 says: "Behold, I will do a new thing; now it shall spring forth; shall ye not know it?"

And now it is that the "remember ye not the former things" falls into place. God is calling us from memory to expectancy. The point is not to forget the past blessings. The point is that God's new blessings, God's new things, will transcend the past, even the glory of the Exodus and the Red Sea crossing. God is calling us from memory to expectancy.

The "remember ye no more" can be seen for what it is. And so I don't forget the past, but in the power of Almighty God, I look to a future that will transcend the past. More than that, I expect it. Yes, I'm not just looking for it. I'm expecting it.

Living expectantly means more than just believing in church doctrines. It means more than just passively trusting my life to God. Living expectantly is faith on tiptoe. Living expectantly means believing with God that life is worth living; it means believing that life will never become routine for me. Believing that in God, I will never experience the dullness of the daily. I live in the expectancy that, in my life, God will do a new thing that will transcend what He has done for me in the past.

Living expectantly is faith on tiptoes.

I am so thankful that God's new thing is not like man's. We're well acquainted with man's new thing. The commercials come on every day. Someone walks in a laundromat, and the man says, "May I have that?"

She says, "No, don't take my Tide."

He says, "But I have something better than Tide."

She says, "Can there be anything better than Tide?"

And then he pulls the cover off. "There it is!"

"What is it?"

"New Tide!"

God's got more for you than "New Tide!" God's new thing is a different thing. That's why I don't have to settle for a negative past. And I will not settle for a positive past.

I can face each day, living not like a *pess-optimist*.

You know what a pess-optimist is? A pess-optimist is a person who believes that things are going to work out. But when they do, it'll be too late. Living expectantly is not living like a pess-optimist. Living expectantly is living like an optimist who, when he has worn out his shoes, figures he's just back on his feet. That's living expectantly, because of God's promise of a new thing.

The Scripture describes this new thing as "a way in the wilderness and rivers in the desert" *(Isaiah 43:19, ESV)*, so don't miss the point. The desert is still there. It's God's blessings, God's new thing that will transcend the past. It will not be in the absence of the desert. It will be *in the middle* of the desert.

It ought to comfort your heart, as it does mine, that God has wilderness experience. He has provided clouds for shade, fire for direction, and manna for food. The God that plans a new thing is the God that has a wilderness track record—not just in the absence of the wilderness but right in the middle of it. So can I wake up each day with an excitement? There are things in store for me every day, because God is doing a new thing. It will be a new thing that satisfies my particular need. I believe that in my home, God is doing a new thing; that in my marriage God is doing a new thing; that in my spiritual life, and yours, God is doing a new thing.

God is doing a new thing that satisfies my particular need.

I challenge you to live expectantly. That God will do it for you, and in your home, and in your career, and in your life, and in your church, and in your life experience. God is doing a new thing for you. You can trust it, because God's promise is backed up by God's power.

He was just a little fellow. His mother died when he was just a child. The father, in trying to be mommy and daddy, planned a picnic. The little boy had never been on a picnic. They made their plans, fixed the lunch, packed the car. Then it was time to go to bed before the picnic the next day. The boy couldn't sleep. He tossed and turned, but the excitement got to him. Finally, he got out of bed, and he ran into the room, where his father had already fallen asleep. He shook his father. His father woke up, looked, saw his son, and said, "What are you doing up? What's the matter?"

The boy said, "I can't sleep."

"Why can't you sleep?"

The boy said, "Daddy, I'm excited about tomorrow!"

"Well, son, I'm sure you are. It's going to be a great day, but it won't be great if we don't get some sleep. Why don't you just run down the hall, get back in bed, and get a good night's rest."

The boy trudged off, through the door, down the hall to his room, got in bed, and before long, sleep came—to the father. It wasn't long, however, before the little boy was back, and he was pushing and shoving his father. His father opened his eyes, and harsh words almost blurted out until he saw the expression on the boy's face.

"What's the matter now?" his father asked.

"Daddy, I just want to thank you for tomorrow."

When I think of my past, and the fact that a loving Father would not let me go, and reached down in His divine providence and lifted me off the streets of Harlem . . . when I think of what he has done for me, and then think that He is planning a new thing for me that will surpass the past, I want the record to show, here and now, Benjamin Reaves testifies, "Father, I want to thank you for tomorrow."

I challenge you to live expectantly, that God will do His new thing in your life, in your home, and in your experience. As a consequence, your grateful testimony should be, "Father, I want to thank you for tomorrow."

Chapter Seventeen

OPPORTUNITY IN OPPOSITION

S LOWLY GLITTERING AND SHIM-
mering, the ball descended from the heights
of Times Square as the screaming mass of
humanity began to count off the seconds to a new
year—a new year that would be another heartbeat
in the pulse of time, a new year that would be an
uncharted path through an unknown future.

What would it be? Some would say, with
thankfulness, "It's a blank page." Some of us
would say with great appreciation, "It's the land
of beginning again." Some of us would say, "It's
a land of opportunity." God knows that, for
all of us, whenever we look back over the past,
and then look forward by God's grace into the

future, the opportunity of beginning again is a welcome one.

> "An open door has been set before me, and never mind the adversaries"
>
> 1Cor. 16:9, Reaves paraphrase

That motivating sense of future and opportunity is what takes me back to a passage that means much to me, to words that Paul proclaimed about another opportunity: "Because a great door for effective work has opened to me, and there are many who oppose me" *(1 Corinthians 16:9, NIV).* Paul wrote these words when he was nearing the close of his ministry in Ephesus. Scripture reveals that, though he decided to move on to Macedonia and then visit the church of Corinth, he couldn't escape a sense of conviction that God had given him for Ephesus: "a great door has opened to me."

A strategic link between east and west, Ephesus was a gateway between the continents. For Paul, Ephesus was an open door for service, for teaching, and for preaching the gospel. He saw in Ephesus a door of opportunity, and in a profound way we all stand at the Ephesus of an open door, an open door set before us by the Lord. It is true for us, as it was true for Paul at Ephesus. In addition it was also true for Paul, as the verse continues, that there were many "who opposed him."

Ephesus, a place of opposition for Paul, was the most magnificent and simultaneously the most corrupt city in Asia. In Ephesus could be found the vast system of organized idolatry to the goddess Diana, where crowds of wandering multitudes, practicing magic and surrendering to sensual and demonic possession, were steeped in intense religious prejudice. All of these were found at Ephesus as Paul testified about the challenges he faced. "There are many who oppose me" and yet, in the same verse he says, "A great door for effective work has opened to me."

It's a strange attitude. It's almost like saying, "I have been given a great opportunity and never mind the adversaries."

What's going on here? Paul is speaking of two contrasting realities. He's talking about the inextricable linkage of opportunity and opposition. *Opportunity, opposition*—the words start out alike, but it's the ending that differs and makes them different, almost contradictory, terms. Paul, like his Lord, made frequent use of metaphors, so he had written indicating that since there were many adversaries, opposition could be expected.

Why would Paul set up that kind of sequence: opportunity, then opposition? The more I studied the passage, the more I understood that he didn't just find opposition at Ephesus, and he didn't just find opportunity at Ephesus.

Instead (and don't miss this)—*he found opportunity in opposition.*

We all stand at the Ephesus of an open door. What lies ahead for you, for me? To attempt to answer that is to be like the student in the classroom after the professor was asking a particularly difficult question. He asked one student, and the student just shrugged his shoulders. Then he asked another student, who said, "I don't know." Then he asked a third student, who cleared his throat and said, "Well, professor, it seems to me that it is clear that I have nothing to add to what has already been said."

It's like that when we talk about what lies ahead because, when I listen to all of the prophets on television speculate about the future, I feel impressed to say: "I don't think I can add anything to what's already been said, because they haven't said anything anyway."

Or, perhaps, I could say this: "I don't know

exactly what the future holds, but I do know that you will find opportunity and you will find opposition."

The cogent question is, Will you find opportunity in opposition? And that's because there's going to be opposition. There will be the opposition of uncontrollable circumstances. There will be the opposition of people; the opposition of your own personality; the opposition of your personal temperament; the opposition of your fears, your ego. There will be the opposition of financial uncertainty, the opposition of career confusion, and the opposition of possible failure.

> God doesn't work through
> us because we're flawless;
> rather, He works through us
> in spite of our imperfections.
> Aiden Wilson Tozer

There will be opposition, and the real question that presses home is, how many open doors will you pass by because of the opposition? How many opportunities will you give up on because of opposition?

In every area of life, organizational and

otherwise, from professional to personal, from secular to spiritual, we all struggle with the inextricable linkage of opportunity and opposition. But I am convinced that this passage, this metaphor of the open door, brings good news for the uncharted journey. This passage sounds a trumpet blast of courage and renewal for our faltering lives because, in this passage, Paul shares with us the secret for finding opportunity in opposition.

> Legacy isn't about us.
> It's about God working
> through us for His glory,
> not ours.
> Charles R. Swindoll

And that secret, in the first hint of this sequence, surfaces in the strange content of the text itself. It does seem strange that Paul would couple together the phrase "great opportunity" with the phrase "there are many against me."

The truth is, many of us would argue that our best work could be done without opposition. How many times have we said, "You know, if it weren't for this" or, "You know, if they weren't doing that" or, "You know, if I just had such and such," and on and on. But Paul wasn't taking that road. Instead, he knew life for what it is: no alibi, and no wistful, wishful thinking. He knew that difficulty and opportunity go hand in hand. He knew that trouble is the doorknob of the open door. Paul had discovered that the first step in finding opportunity in opposition is to accept the fact that, in the living of life, opportunity and opposition walk together.

"A great opportunity and many against me." This means that we have to face up to life as it is, and not as we wish it to be.

As I have discovered, there will be opposition, and I must also recognize that the opposition sometimes is me. Jean and I had been married for two years and were living in Terre Haute, Indiana, where I was assisting in an evangelistic meeting. I was scheduled to preach on a Sunday night, but as the week drew near I was busy with a lot of little things when Jean inquired, "Shouldn't you be studying your sermon?"

Patiently I explained to her I had attended seminary and received an A in homiletics and everything was under control.

Her response was, "What!" followed by a look that said, "Are you out of your mind?"

Well, it seems God felt the same way and

decided remedial action was needed, so He let me have the service and the sermon all by myself. It was an unmitigated disaster, and yes, it was a scalpel moment. Ever since that experience, on the inside cover of my Bible is my handwritten reminder, "I bring my best to the Lord, but the battle is the Lord's."

Life is not a never-never land. And I hate to disillusion you, but there's no Mickey Mouse, no Minnie Mouse, and no Donald Duck. Life is good and life is hard. Life is promising and life can be depressing. Life is hopeful and life can be despairing. There's opportunity and there's opposition. One of the mysterious truths of this world is that God so allowed that nothing comes but at the price of effort. We need a willingness to face competition, to face difficulty, to face adversaries, to face opposition. Nothing comes without struggle, even in the Christian life, because the Christian life advances by overcoming.

Yes, there is the opposition, but don't lose sight of the fact that for Paul the presence of the opposition does not lessen the excitement and the attraction of the opportunity. In the text, Paul rejoices over a God-opened door. Indeed, the many adversaries, the opposition, were all part of the opportunity. Opposition can often be commensurate with the opportunity.

Yes, you've got a great opportunity ahead of you, but, yes, you have great opposition ahead of you too. The opposition is often commensurate with the opportunity, but maybe the secret to finding opportunity in opposition is to accept the fact that they walk together.

Or can it be that the secret in finding opportunity in opposition is to reset the focus from the negative to the positive. *The open door has been set before me; never mind the adversaries.* Now, to be fair and realistic and not Pollyanna-ish: opposition does not automatically add up to opportunity. It depends on your focus.

I remember buying some property in Huntsville, Alabama, a few years back. People came out to check the property boundaries, and they told me that metal stakes had been driven into the soil to mark the boundaries of my property.

Over the passage of years, soil and grass had covered the stakes, so they used metal detectors to try to determine what those boundaries were. I watched in fascination as they would take the metal detector and move it around, and then, all of a sudden, a little buzz would arise from the device. They would stop searching and start digging. I remember one time I watched them dig and dig and, finally when they finished digging, they came up with a beer can.

Many of us are like metal detectors. We can detect under layer and layer of opportunity a beer can of opposition. We see everything in negative terms, the terms of opposition. We focus on what can go wrong. We fret and worry about what has not yet happened.

Thus, to be able to find opportunity in opposition, we need to reset the focus. This is not to deny the negative but, rather, to give priority to the positive. Note the way the verse reads, the flow of thought. It starts off with the opportunity, "an open door," and then it moves on to the opposition, "many adversaries."

Suppose Paul had written it in a different way? Suppose Paul had written it the way we might have written it? Suppose the verse said: "The opposition is fierce, but of course there's some opportunity here too"?

Can you see the crucial difference here? That would be a different emphasis. We've got to reset the focus.

It's as if I took a six-inch-wide plank and laid it out across some chairs, and then announced that I would give a thousand dollars to anybody that would walk across that plank from one chair to the other. I'd have to get out of the way because people would trample me trying to get to that plank. But if I put up some scaffolding twenty feet off the ground, laid the plank across the scaffolding, and then said: "I'll give a thousand dollars to anyone who will walk across this plank," a lot fewer would do it, right? That's because when the plank is only three feet from the ground, you would be focusing on the prize, but when it's up twenty feet in the air, you'd be focusing on the penalty.

Storms can also bring out courage, a soul strength that is absolutely awesome because courage can grow out of fear.

Thus, we must reset the focus. That's why Paul wrote it the way he did, and not the way we might have. Paul is saying, "An open door has been set before me, and *never mind* the adversaries." Resetting the focus enables us to shift the center of our lives to where oppositions will become opportunities. It enables us to shift the center of our lives to where opposition can bring out the best in us.

I've read of the trees that live above the timberline. That timberline is the point of unrestrained winds, the point where trees have to fight for their existence. It is said that the wood of such trees has a certain toughness about it. It has a strength and a musical quality that's not found in wood grown lower down. In the human experience, we every now and then find ourselves living at the timberline, nakedly exposed to fears and storms. Trying to stand up beneath harsh winds that test every fiber of our being can be hard, but it also can bring out a toughness in us that otherwise might never exist.

Storms can also bring out courage, a soul strength that is absolutely awesome because courage can grow out of fear. Kindness grows out of suffering. Endurance grows out of burdens, and compassion grows out of tears. That can be because of a focus that finds opportunity in opposition.

But there is a third element in all this, and it's one that that we must not forget. And that is continuing faith in our God.

"The open door has been set before me." In the Greek, it's in the perfect tense, which means it sets forth the completed work. Paul is saying: "The door stands open, the Lord opened it, and the

Lord keeps it open for me." No wonder, this is the Paul who proclaims from his dungeon, "I know in whom I believed." This is the Paul who could say: "I'm confident. I am convinced that Christianity is more than a new life. It's a new power." That is because Christianity gives us a confident faith, not in the absence of adversaries, but a faith in God's direction, in God's provision, and in God's providence—no matter the adversaries. "The open door has been set before me."

> When God gives opportunity, He provides resources.

It was about nine o'clock a.m., and I stood waiting for a store to open. I stood staring at the door, and the closed door stared back at me. I turned to look around to see what was going on around me. When I turned back, the door was still there staring at me.

As I stood there, a man walked by me, walked up to the door, and the door opened. Clearly, some doors appear closed until you advance, and unless you advance, it doesn't matter if the door is open or closed. The point is that springs of triumph bubble up not out of friendly circumstances but out of God-given resources, whatever the circumstances happen to be.

When God gives opportunity, He provides resources. That's why in this text you don't hear Paul asking for pity. This is not a pity party. He sees opposition as evidence that this is a divine opportunity, and he's not going to let anything rob him of that opportunity. All through his ministry he had experienced what trials could do to him, but more importantly, he knew what they could *not* do. He knew, as we need to know, that the Christian life proceeds in spite of opposition, and it proceeds in spite of consequences.

> Jesus took the cross, a symbol of shame, and made it a symbol of triumph.

"The open door has been set before me, and never mind the adversaries."

That's tough talk. To talk like that, you need to have access to a spiritual bank account that you can draw on, the bank account of one who from the wood of the cross fashioned a grand and glorious door—an open door. He took the cross, a symbol of shame, and made it a symbol of triumph. His life proclaims that an open door is set before me and is set before you—never mind the adversaries.

So what will the future hold? What will it be for you? What will it be for me? Maybe you had a tough go in the past? Maybe you got off on the wrong foot? Maybe, if you think about it, you really don't know how you survived. Maybe, if you're willing to confess it, you would admit that the turbulent waters of temptation have washed away the foundations of your moral resolve. Maybe you would confess that the resulting flood meant your spiritual life should be declared a disaster area.

I don't know what you do see when you look back. I speak only to what you can see as you look forward to the open door set before you.

Whatever the past may be, straighten up your back, hold up your head, blink back the tears, stiffen your resolve, and determine by God's grace to be relentlessly faithful and ruthlessly fearless, claiming your God-given opportunity and an open door that has been set before you.

Scripture makes it clear it was not in their own power that the apostles accomplished their mission, but in the power of the living God. Their work was not easy. Familiar companions for them were hardship and bitter grief, privation and persecution, but they were willing to spend and be spent. They enjoyed the supreme privilege of omnipotence working through them to make the Gospel triumph.

> The apostles enjoyed the supreme privilege of omnipotence working through them to make the Gospel triumph.

That sacred privilege is ours as well.

My heart overflows with thanksgiving at the marvelous love, the forgiving grace of God, knowing me as He does, intimately acquainted with my past—the secrets, the skeletons, and the shut doors. Undeservedly He will still choose to work through me, and He will work through you, to enable us to find opportunity in opposition.

Chapter
Eighteen

MY SCALPEL MOMENTS

AS WE'VE JOURNEYED TOGETHER through the pages of this book, my prayer is that you've come to understand and perhaps even embrace those occasions in life that I call "Scalpel Moments." Those unexpected, unanticipated moments when an encounter, a word, a comment, a look, a realization, or a divine intrusion—like an extremely sharp scalpel—removes from our lives things we are better off without. Things such as attitudes, obsessions, options, or behaviors that can hide the "better you."

This brings us to a transition point. Now that you have read the stories of biblical and contemporary characters having their *Scalpel Moments*, what will you do next? What will you do with the insights you've gained. How will you apply them to your life? Can you recognize your own Scalpel Moments from the past? Moments that, while painful, may have caused you to grow and become a better person?

I don't want you to miss this moment. I don't want you to leave this book unchanged. So let me give you an opportunity. A chance to write a chapter in this book from your own life experience. This is an opportunity for reflection and renewal. A chance to consider your past and log the *Scalpel Moments* in your life that loom large like mileposts of memory.

Why write them in this book? Because in years to come you may return to these pages for comfort, guidance or insight. When you open the book again, the familiar stories you've just read will still be here waiting to inspire you again. But in addition, your own story will be recorded here. And that, I believe, may provide you the greatest encouragement of them all.

So take a few moments now to journal your journey. Don't put it off till later. If it helps you, think of the remainder of this chapter like a personal diary. Pages where you can recall, remember, review, revisit, and record Scalpel Moments in your life.

Consider how God shaped you from what you used to be, to what you are now. My prayer is that these memories will remind you of God's goodness and give you a new commitment to "grow in the grace and knowledge of our Lord and Savior Jesus Christ" (2 Peter 3:18 NIV).

MY SCALPEL MOMENTS

_____

_____

_____

_____

_____

_____

_____

_____

_____

_____

_____

_____

_____

_____

_____

_____

_____

_____

_____

_____

_____

_____

_____

_____

_____

_____

_____

_____

_____

_____

_____

_____

_____

_____

_____

_____

_____

_____

_____

_____

_____

_____

_____

_____

_____

_____

_____

_____

_____

_____

_____

_____

_____

_____

_____

_____

_____

_____

_____

_____

_____

_____

Epilogue:
MOMENTS OF GRACE

FROM HOLLYWOOD HENDERson the throes of anguish, to King David rebuked for sin, from Dr. Benjamin Reaves on the streets of Harlem, NY, to the apostle Paul facing opposition, we have looked at various situations in human life. We have seen successes and disasters, triumphs and failures. But amid it all, if nothing else, I hope we have seen the reality of God's grace working in the lives of fallen, sinful, defective people, such as myself. A sinner saved by grace, the grace of a God who, through various scalpel moments, has changed, and is still changing, my life.

And that's because God is a God who wants to forgive, to heal, to restore, and to redeem. That's why, all through the Bible, God is depicted as a forgiving God, a healing God, a restoring God, and a redeeming One as well.

And a great example of what our God is like is with Peter, whom we saw earlier, first messing up in Jerusalem, when he denied Jesus three times, and then later, in Antioch, when he forgot the reality of the grace bestowed even to him.

And yet, what? The same Peter who denied Jesus three times was the same Peter to whom Jesus later said, "Feed my sheep" *(John 21:17, NIV)*, the same Peter who was to write crucial books in the New Testament. In other words, though he faced some rough moments, some scalpel moments, Peter was forgiven, healed, restored, and redeemed. That is, they were not just scalpel moments; they were, truly, moments of grace as well.

That's what our God is all about—grace, and my hope and prayer is that, from having read this book, you will experience for yourself the reality of God's grace, even if it takes a few scalpel moments to get you there.

A fellow traveler,
Benjamin Reaves

End Notes

1. "The Quote Garden," Usman B. Asif, last modified Feb 3, 2016, quotegarden.com.

2. David Roper, *Our Daily Bread*, Nov 4, 2003, Daily Bread Ministries.

3. Ellen G. White, *Conflict and Courage* (Hagerstown, MD: Ellen G. White Estate Inc., 2000), 179.

4. This popular quotation (along with numerous variations) is sometimes attributed to Francis of Assisi. As of this writing, no published source prior to 1990 has been found to verify that this is indeed an original Assisi quotation. However, since no one else to date has laid claim to these marvelous words, I will leave the attribution as it stands.

5. Ellen G. White, *Thoughts from the Mount of Blessing*, (Nampa: Pacific Press Publishing Association, 1999), 36.

6. John R. W. Stott, *Christian Counterculture*, 63, 65.

7. John R. W. Stott, *The Message of the Sermon on the Mount*, (Downers Grove: Intervarsity Press, 1978), 55.

8. Ellen G. White, *Selected Messages Book 2*, (Hagerstown: Review and Herald Publishing Association, 2007), 155.

9. Ellen G. White, *The Spirit of Prophecy*, Volume 2, 214.

Acknowledgments

B ECAUSE MY LIFE JOURNEY
started in the wise providence of God,
gratitude for His guidance opens my
heartfelt acknowledgments. Closely following is
thanks for and to my loving parents, Ernest and
Lella Reaves. They provided a home setting that
nurtured and inspired me and my siblings Ernest,
Robert, and Edith. I have been blessed by my
children Terrilyn, Pamela, Benjamin Jr, and the
grandchildren Marcia, Shanika and Keon for
their enthusiastic encouragement.

My journey in ministry, higher education,
and healthcare calls forth appreciation for all
the mentors, ministers, educators, administrators

and colleagues who have poured into my life. Giants like E. E. Cleveland, Charles Bradford, E. C. Ward, Mardian Blair, and Tom Werner. In addition is special thanks in abundance to Don Jernigan, whose leadership I respect and whose friendship I treasure. His support and encouragement for this project was incalculable. Recognition is more than appropriate for Shirley Iheanacho, and Roy Malcolm for their persistent motivation.

I am keenly cognizant of my indebtedness to Todd Chobotar, publisher and editor, who expanded and informed my vision of the project, as well as the skillful, patient assistance of Lillian Boyd and the team of editors and photographers.

I conclude these acknowledgments by traveling back over the years to 1953, and across the miles to Huntsville, Alabama at then Oakwood College. There is where I met "my beautiful brown-eyed Jean." Her love embraced me as I was, supported me on the journey to what I could be and encouraged the best in me for the fifty-eight years of our married life.

DR. BENJAMIN F. Reaves now serves as special advisor for mission and ministries to the president of Adventist Health System. He joined Adventist Health System in April of 1997 as vice president of ministries. Prior to this position, he served as general field secretary for the General Conference of Seventh-day Adventists. Previously, Dr. Reaves served for eleven years as the ninth president of Oakwood College. A native of New York City, he received a BA from Oakwood College (1955); MA in religion from Andrews University (1966); MDiv from Andrews University (1972); and a DMin from Chicago Theological Seminary (1974). In 1987 Dr. Reaves received a diploma for completion of the Harvard University Institute in Educational Management, Cambridge, Mass.

Before assuming his position as president of Oakwood College, Dr. Reaves was chairman for the Department of Religion and Theology at Oakwood College for eight years. He has also held the following positions: associate professor of preaching and urban ministry, Seventh-day Adventist Theological Seminary; campus pastor for college youth, Andrews University; and pastor evangelist for both the Michigan Conference and Lake Region Conference. Reaves was the first African American to chair the world church nominating committee at the general conference session in Utrecht. He has served as visiting professor, Andrews University and the Chicago Cluster of Theological Seminaries. Dr. Reaves is the first Adventist elected to serve as chairman of the member presidents of the United Negro College Fund, as well as vice-chair of the UNCF Corporate Board of Directors and its Executive Committee. He also served as vice-chair of NAFEO, the National Association for Equal Opportunity in Higher Education.

Dr. Reaves is a recipient of the Distinguished Alumnus Award at Oakwood College, the Crystal Angel Award from Adventist Health System, and has also received the Adventist Education

Medallion of Distinction, the highest award conferred jointly by the Education Department of the General Conference and the world divisions to outstanding Adventist educators. He was one of the first three African Americans voted into the Huntsville, Alabama, Rotary Club. Reaves is widely published and has received numerous awards and honors. He is a member of the Academy of Homiletics and was listed by the US Army Board of Chaplains to conduct workshops in homiletics and liturgies.

He is a world traveler, preaching and lecturing throughout the Caribbean, Bermuda, England, Canada, Europe, Australia, South Africa, as well as the United States. For twenty-one years he has been a featured speaker for the Chicago Sunday Evening Club television broadcast.

On that journey, Dr. Reaves was married for fifty-eight years to the love of his life, the former Jean Manuel, now deceased. She served as assistant professor at Oakwood College for fashion merchandising and interior design. They were blessed with three children, Terrilyn Jackson, Benjamin Jr., and Pamela Walker, and three grandchildren.

ABOUT THE PUBLISHER

For over one hundred years the mission of Florida Hospital has been: To extend the healing ministry of Christ. Opened in 1908, Florida Hospital is comprised of nine hospital campuses housing over 2,700 beds and twenty-three walk-in medical centers. With over 20,000 employees—including 2,200 doctors and 6,600 nurses—Florida Hospital serves the residents and guests of Orlando, the No. 1 tourist destination in the world. Florida Hospital has over 2 million patient visits a year. Florida Hospital is a Christian, faith-based hospital that believes in providing Whole Person Care to all patients – mind, body, and spirit. Hospital fast facts include:

LARGEST ADMITTING HOSPITAL IN AMERICA.
Ranked No. 1 in the nation for inpatient admissions by the American Hospital Association.

AMERICA'S HEART HOSPITAL.
Ranked No. 1 in the nation for number of heart procedures performed each year, averaging 20,000 cases annually. MSNBC named Florida Hospital "America's Heart Hospital" for being the No. 1 hospital fighting America's No. 1 killer—heart disease.

ONE OF AMERICA'S BEST HOSPITALS.
Recognized by *U.S. News & World Report* as "One of America's Best Hospitals" for ten years. Clinical specialties recognized have included: Cardiology & Heart Surgery, Orthopaedics, Neurology & Neuroscience, Urology, Gynecology, Gastroenterology & GI Surgery, Diabetes and Endocrinology, Pulmonology, Nephrology, and Geriatrics.

HOSPITAL OF THE FUTURE.
At the turn of the century, the Wall Street Journal named Florida Hospital the "Hospital of the Future".

LEADER IN SENIOR CARE.
Florida Hospital serves the largest number of seniors in America through Medicare with a goal for each patient to experience a "Century of Health" by living to a healthy hundred.

TOP BIRTHING CENTER.
Fit Pregnancy magazine named Florida Hospital one of the "Top 10 Best Places in the Country to have a Baby". As a result, The Discovery Health Channel struck a three-year production deal with Florida Hospital to host a live broadcast called "Birth Day Live." Florida Hospital annually delivers over 10,000 babies.

CORPORATE ALLIANCES.
Florida Hospital maintains corporate alliance relationships with a select group of Fortune 500 companies including Disney, Nike, Johnson & Johnson, Philips, AGFA, and Stryker.

DISNEY PARTNERSHIP.

Florida Hospital is the Central Florida health & wellness resource of the Walt Disney World® Resort. Florida Hospital also partnered with Disney to build the ground breaking health and wellness facility called Florida Hospital Celebration Health located in Disney's town of Celebration, Florida. Disney and Florida Hospital recently partnered to build a new state-of-the-art Children's Hospital.

HOSPITAL OF THE 21ST CENTURY.

Florida Hospital Celebration Health was awarded the Premier Patient Services Innovator Award as "The Model for Healthcare Delivery in the 21st Century".

CONSUMER CHOICE AWARD WINNER.

Florida Hospital has received the Consumer Choice Award from the National Research Corporation every year from 1996 to the present.

SPORTS EXPERTS.

Florida Hospital is the official hospital of the Orlando Magic NBA basketball team. In addition, Florida Hospital has an enduring track record of providing exclusive medical care to many sports organizations. These organizations have included: Disney's Wide World of Sports, Walt Disney World's Marathon Weekend, the Capital One Bowl, and University of Central Florida Athletics. Florida Hospital has also provided comprehensive healthcare services for the World Cup and Olympics.

PUBLICATIONS.

Florida Hospital Publishing can help you live life to the fullest with a variety of health and wellness books and other resources uniquely focused on Whole Person Health. Visit: FloridaHospitalPublishing.com

FLORIDA HOSPITAL

The skill to heal. The spirit to care.®

601 E. Rollins Street, Orlando, FL 32803
FloridaHospital.org | (407) 303-5600

LEAD YOUR COMMUNITY
TO HEALTHY
LIVING

Seminar Leader Kit
Everything a leader needs to conduct this seminar successfully, including key questions to facilitate group discussion and PowerPoint™ presentations for each of the eight principles.

Participant Guide
A study guide with essential information from each of the eight lessons along with outlines, self assessments, and questions for people to fill in as they follow along.

Small Group Kit
It's easy to lead a small group using the CREATION Health videos, the Small Group Leaders Guide, and the Small Group Discussion Guide.

INCLUDES
ONLINE TRAINING

CREATION HEALTH RESOURCES

CREATION Kids
CREATION Health Kids can make a big difference in homes, schools, and congregations. Lead kids in your community to healthier, happier living.

Bible Stories
God is interested in our physical, mental and spiritual well-being. Throughout the Bible you can discover the eight principles for full life.

Life Guide Series
These guides include questions designed to help individuals or small groups study the depths of every principle and learn strategies for integrating them into everyday life.

CREATION Health Devotional for Women
Written for women by women, the CREATION Health Devotional for Women is based on the principles of whole-person wellness represented in CREATION Health. Spirits will be lifted and lives rejuvenated by the message of each unique chapter.

CREATION Health One-Sentence Journal
(Hardcover, small gift-size)

The CREATION Health One-SENTENCE Journal is a simple, fun, and powerful tool to transform your life. It takes just moments a day. Yet the effect it can have over time is life-changing.

CREATION Health Discovery
Written by Des Cummings Jr., PhD, Monica Reed, MD, and Todd Chobotar, this wonderful resource introduces people to the CREATION Health philosophy and lifestyle.

CREATION Health Devotional (English: Hardcover / Spanish: Softcover)
In this devotional you will discover stories about experiencing God's grace in the tough times, God's delight in triumphant times, and God's presence in peaceful times.

ADDITIONAL RESOURCES

The Hidden Power of Relentless Stewardship (Hardcover)
Dr. Jernigan shows how an organization's culture can be molded to create high performance at every level, fulfilling mission and vision, while wisely utilizing - or stewarding - the limited resources of time, money, and energy.

Leadership in the Crucible of Work (Hardcover)

What is the first and most important work of a leader? (The answer may surprise you.) In *Leadership in the Crucible of Work*, noted speaker, poet, and college president Dr. Sandy Shugart takes readers on an unforgettable journey to the heart of what it means to become an authentic leader.

Growing Physician Leaders (Hardcover)
Retired Army Lieutenant General Mark Hertling applies his four decades of military leadership to the work of healthcare, resulting in a profoundly constructive and practical book with the power to reshape and re-energize any healthcare organization in America today.

CREATION Health Breakthrough (Hardcover)

Blending science and lifestyle recommendations, Monica Reed, MD, prescribes eight essentials that will help reverse harmful health habits and prevent disease. Discover how intentional choices, rest, environment, activity, trust, relationships, outlook, and nutrition can put a person on the road to wellness.

Forgive To Live (English: Hardcover/Spanish: Softcover)
In *Forgive To Live: How Forgiveness Can Save Your Life*, Dr. Tibbits presents the scientifically proven steps for forgiveness—taken from the first clinical study of its kind conducted by Stanford University and Florida Hospital.

Forgive To Live Devotional (Hardcover)

In his powerful new devotional, Dr. Dick Tibbits reveals the secret to forgiveness. This compassionate devotional is a stirring look at the true meaning of forgiveness. Each of the fifty-six spiritual insights include motivational Scripture, an inspirational prayer, and two thought-provoking questions. The insights are designed to encourage your journey as you begin to *Forgive to Live*.

ADDITIONAL RESOURCES

The Love Fight (Softcover)
Are you going to fight for love or against each other? The authors illustrate how this common encounter can create a mutually satisfying relationship. Their expertise will walk you through the scrimmage between those who want to accomplish and those who want to relate.

Health & Healing Bible Promise Book (Hardcover)
The Bible is packed with promises on health and healing - from aging to nutrition to rest, from grief to anger to stress. The *Health & Healing Bible Promise Book* collects over 600 scriptures in more than thirty different translations in a convenient pocket size on these topics and more including the CREATION Health principles.

Pain Free For Life (Hardcover)
In *Pain Free For Life*, Scott C. Brady, MD,—founder of Florida Hospital's Brady Institute for Health—leads pain-racked readers to a pain-free life using powerful mind-body-spirit strategies —where more than 80 percent of his chronic-painpatients have achieved 80–100 percent pain relief within weeks.

Supersized Kids (Hardcover)
In *SuperSized Kids: How to Rescue Your Child from The Obesity Threat*, Walt Larimore, MD, and Sherri Flynt, MPH, R.D, L.D, explains step by step, how parents can work to avert the coming childhood obesity crisis by taking control of the weight challenges facing

If Today Is All I Have
At its heart, Linda's captivating account chronicles the struggle to reconcile her three dreams of experiencing life as a "normal woman" with the tough realities of her medical condition. Her journey is punctuated with insights that are at times humorous, painful, provocative, and life-affirming.

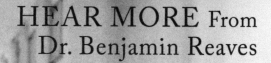

HEAR MORE From
Dr. Benjamin Reaves

LET DR. REAVES LEAD YOUR TEAM THROUGH THE JOURNEY OF SCALPEL MOMENTS

DR. REAVES SPEAKS ON MANY TOPICS INCLUDING:

- Opportunity in Opposition
  How Adversity Leads to God's Open Door

- Living Expectantly
  Going Beyond Your Limitations of the Past

- Journey Towards the Crucial Conversation
  Encounters with God

- Christian Discipleship
  From Prison to Celebration